Especially for

....

From

....

Date

....

My Prayer
JOURNAL

———— ◆ ————

Bible Encouragement for
Hope & Healing

BARBOUR BOOKS
An Imprint of Barbour Publishing, Inc.

© 2019 by Barbour Publishing

Written and compiled by Karin Dahl Silver.

ISBN 978-1-68322-758-8

Some text originally appeared in *The Bible Promise Book* for Hope and Healing.
Published by Barbour Publishing, Inc.

All scripture quotations are taken from the King James Version of the Bible.

Published by Barbour Books, an imprint of Barbour Publishing, Inc., 1810 Barbour Drive, Uhrichsville, Ohio 44683, www.barbourbooks.com

Our mission is to inspire the world with the life-changing message of the Bible.

Member of the
Evangelical Christian
Publishers Association

Printed in China.

Contents

Introduction

Whatever the need of the moment, the answer can be found in scripture—if we take the time to seek it out. Whatever we're feeling, whatever we're suffering, whatever we're hoping, the Bible has something to say to us.

This collection of prayers, Bible verses, and devotional thoughts is meant for use as an inspiration for your daily prayer needs—especially when you need encouragement on a particular problem in your life.

If, for example, you are struggling with depression or loneliness, shame or worry, some of the Bible's promises are available to you in these pages. You'll find carefully selected verses for fifty topics dealing with hope and healing, arranged alphabetically for ease of use.

We hope it will be an encouragement to you as you record your heartfelt prayers to God, who promises to hear every word.

And this is the confidence that we have in him,
that, if we ask any thing according
to his will, he heareth us.

1 John 5:14

Abuse

◆

Abuse, in whatever form it takes, is completely against God's just and loving nature. His Word speaks out repeatedly against the wickedness of oppression—harming others with violent actions and words. An abuse survivor has a long, difficult road to walk, but your God will go with you—no amount of pain you carry is too difficult for Him. He invites you to pour out your heart; He can fill you with His truth and peace to answer the shame and guilt you might feel. These Bible promises show that the almighty God is powerful to defend and restore you.

The LORD also will be a refuge for the oppressed,
a refuge in times of trouble. And they that know
thy name will put their trust in thee: for thou,
LORD, hast not forsaken them that seek thee.

PSALM 9:9–10

Father, You know the pain I carry in my heart, in my body, in my memories. My soul cries out for justice. Help me cling to You, for You are the only one who is truly just. Fill me with the deep-down assurance that You will work what is right.

....

....

....

....

....

....

....

....

....

....

....

....

Strengthen ye the weak hands, and confirm the feeble knees.
Say to them that are of a fearful heart, Be strong, fear not:
behold, your God will come with vengeance, even God
with a recompence; he will come and save you.

ISAIAH 35:3–4

For he hath not despised nor abhorred the affliction
of the afflicted; neither hath he hid his face from him;
but when he cried unto him, he heard.

PSALM 22:24

It feels like so much has been stolen from me—
peace, safety, loving relationships without fear. But You,
Faithful God, promise to heal and restore me. Your everlasting
love is a safe haven, a tower of strength. Please lead me to
friendships and relationships that reflect Your love for me.

....

....

....

....

....

....

....

....

....

....

A father of the fatherless, and a judge of the widows,
is God in his holy habitation. God setteth the solitary in families:
he bringeth out those which are bound with chains:
but the rebellious dwell in a dry land.

PSALM 68:5–6

And I will restore to you the years that the locust hath eaten,
the cankerworm, and the caterpiller, and the palmerworm, my great
army which I sent among you. And ye shall eat in plenty, and be
satisfied, and praise the name of the LORD your God, that hath dealt
wondrously with you: and my people shall never be ashamed.

JOEL 2:25–26

Father, how could my abuser treat me like that and claim they cared for me? I don't know how to forgive them. Bring Your perfect justice; protect my heart from bitterness, and bind up its deep wounds. Holy Spirit, thank You for praying on my behalf when I have no words left.

....

....

....

....

....

....

....

....

....

....

When my father and my mother forsake me,
then the LORD will take me up.

PSALM 27:10

Likewise the Spirit also helpeth our infirmities: for we know not what we should pray for as we ought: but the Spirit itself maketh intercession for us with groanings which cannot be uttered. And he that searcheth the hearts knoweth what is the mind of the Spirit, because he maketh intercession for the saints according to the will of God.

ROMANS 8:26–27

Addiction

⬩

For those who struggle with overcoming addiction, take heart in these truths. Our God is stronger than anything that holds power over us. No matter how far we fall, God can always reach down to us and lift us up. His grace and forgiveness are greater than any amount of temptation or relapses we might experience. The Almighty is near and ready to help. These Bible promises show that Jesus has already won the victory over anything that entangles us. Moving forward in His freedom, we can learn to love and worship Him with all our hearts and our strength.

If the Son therefore shall make you free,
ye shall be free indeed.

John 8:36

Jesus, temptations surround me, whispering promises to satisfy my wants and needs—but after coming this far, I know they will only leave me in misery. I run to You for help; deliver me from them! I lean my whole self on Your faithfulness, Your strength, for You will never fail me.

....

....

....

....

....

....

....

....

....

....

There hath no temptation taken you but such as is common to man: but God is faithful, who will not suffer you to be tempted above that ye are able; but will with the temptation also make a way to escape, that ye may be able to bear it.

1 CORINTHIANS 10:13

But I see another law in my members, warring against the law of my mind, and bringing me into captivity to the law of sin which is in my members. O wretched man that I am! who shall deliver me from the body of this death? I thank God through Jesus Christ our Lord.

ROMANS 7:23–25

Lord Jesus, when I trusted in Your gift of salvation, You broke sin's power over me. But temptation is still present. Proclaim Your liberty to me again, as many times as I need. Strengthen my heart to walk in the Spirit, for I choose to follow You.

....

....

....

....

....

....

....

....

....

....

....

The Spirit of the Lord GOD is upon me; because the LORD hath anointed me to preach good tidings unto the meek; he hath sent me to bind up the brokenhearted, to proclaim liberty to the captives, and the opening of the prison to them that are bound.

ISAIAH 61:1

This I say then, Walk in the Spirit, and ye shall not fulfil the lust of the flesh. For the flesh lusteth against the Spirit, and the Spirit against the flesh: and these are contrary the one to the other: so that ye cannot do the things that ye would. . . . And they that are Christ's have crucified the flesh with the affections and lusts.

GALATIANS 5:16–17, 24

Anger

On our healing journey, we might have a million reasons to be angry. We're furious at people who have hurt us deeply. We grow frustrated at our bodies' slow healing or the onslaught of bad news from our doctors. While anger burns bright, its heat cannot heal. Anger can quickly reduce our hearts to ashes and cultivate a rich growing place for bitterness. God can help us with the anger we feel. He is gracious to listen, to forgive, and to work peace within us. These Bible promises show that though anger is powerful, God's healing can overcome its harm.

Wherefore, my beloved brethren, let every man be swift to hear, slow to speak, slow to wrath: for the wrath of man worketh not the righteousness of God.

JAMES 1:19–20

Your Word is clear, Father—the words I speak come from what is within my heart. I know this anger does not please You, and though it feels good now, it will only harm me in the long run. Cleanse and renew my heart so my mouth can glorify You.

....

....

....

....

....

....

....

....

....

....

Create in me a clean heart, O God; and renew a right spirit within me. Cast me not away from thy presence; and take not thy holy spirit from me. Restore unto me the joy of thy salvation; and uphold me with thy free spirit.

PSALM 51:10–12

A good man out of the good treasure of his heart bringeth forth that which is good; and an evil man out of the evil treasure of his heart bringeth forth that which is evil: for of the abundance of the heart his mouth speaketh.

LUKE 6:45

Father, You know about the anger I feel deep inside. I never want it to see the light of day, but it's still there. Help me to put it away: to forgive those who need it, to ask forgiveness when I need it. Help me to extend grace to all, as You do.

....
....
....
....
....
....
....
....
....
....
....
....

What man is he that desireth life, and loveth many days, that he may see good? Keep thy tongue from evil, and thy lips from speaking guile.

PSALM 34:12–13

Let all bitterness, and wrath, and anger, and clamour, and evil speaking, be put away from you, with all malice: and be ye kind one to another, tenderhearted, forgiving one another, even as God for Christ's sake hath forgiven you.

EPHESIANS 4:31–32

I tremble at the brokenness of this world, Holy Creator. Sin's presence brings about all this pain, and I can't help but feel frustrated, furious. Teach me to wait on You, laying these feelings at Your feet. You will make all things new; You will sustain me now and forever.

....
....
....
....
....
....
....
....
....
....
....
....
....

Be ye angry, and sin not: let not the sun go down upon your wrath: neither give place to the devil.
EPHESIANS 4:26–27

Cease from anger, and forsake wrath: fret not thyself in any wise to do evil. For evildoers shall be cut off: but those that wait upon the LORD, they shall inherit the earth.
PSALM 37:8–9

Anxiety

---

*A*nxiety can show up in our bodies in many ways, from sweaty palms to full-blown panic attacks. Whatever its cause—fear, stress, bodily imbalances—we aren't at the mercy of our anxiety. Jesus is near to us in our distress, and in His Word He promises that He knows what we need from Him before we even ask. We can learn to recognize the situations and thoughts that trigger our anxiety or fear and practice bringing those things before our strong Protector. These Bible promises affirm that when we call to Him, He answers our cries with power and peace.

He shall cover thee with his feathers, and under his wings shalt thou trust: his truth shall be thy shield and buckler. Thou shalt not be afraid for the terror by night; nor for the arrow that flieth by day; nor for the pestilence that walketh in darkness; nor for the destruction that wasteth at noonday.

PSALM 91:4–6

Father, no matter the situation I must walk through today, I trust Your Word when You tell me I am safe in Your care and love. When the fears in my heart are racing ahead, remind me that You are near, You are strong, and You promise to help me.

....

....

....

....

....

....

....

....

....

....

....

For I the LORD thy God will hold thy right hand,
saying unto thee, Fear not; I will help thee.
ISAIAH 41:13

Who shall separate us from the love of Christ? shall tribulation, or
distress, or persecution, or famine, or nakedness, or peril, or sword?
As it is written, for thy sake we are killed all the day long; we are
accounted as sheep for the slaughter. Nay, in all these things we are
more than conquerors through him that loved us.
ROMANS 8:35–37

I'm ashamed of my anxieties, Father. It's a daily struggle to do things others find easy. Help me cling to Your promise—You give flourishing life to all who trust You, no matter their struggles. Thank You that I can rest in Your protective shadow and seek refuge in You.

....
....
....
....
....
....
....
....
....
....

Blessed is the man that trusteth in the LORD, and whose hope the LORD is. For he shall be as a tree planted by the waters, and that spreadeth out her roots by the river, and shall not see when heat cometh, but her leaf shall be green; and shall not be careful in the year of drought, neither shall cease from yielding fruit.

JEREMIAH 17:7–8

He that dwelleth in the secret place of the most High shall abide under the shadow of the Almighty. I will say of the LORD, He is my refuge and my fortress: my God; in him will I trust.

PSALM 91:1–2

Blessings

◆

When we're waiting for God to answer the prayers closest to our hearts, we can lose sight of how He shows us love through His daily blessings. He sends us friends who pray for us, the beauty of creation, and faithful reminders in His Word of how we can never be taken out of His hands. It can be hard, but look around you. Find the people and activities that continually breathe life and joy into you in the midst of this difficult time. Meditate on these Bible promises that show how God gives good gifts to His children!

Blessed be the Lord, who daily loadeth us with benefits, even the God of our salvation. Selah.

Psalm 68:19

God of abundance, thank You that You are not stingy with Your blessings, Your love, or Your presence. When I feel too broken or needy to even ask for help, give me eyes to see Your good gifts that come showering from heaven; fill my heart with peace in You.

....

....

....

....

....

....

....

....

....

....

Every good gift and every perfect gift is from above, and cometh down from the Father of lights, with whom is no variableness, neither shadow of turning.

JAMES 1:17

And I will make them and the places round about my hill a blessing; and I will cause the shower to come down in his season; there shall be showers of blessing. And the tree of the field shall yield her fruit, and the earth shall yield her increase, and they shall be safe in their land, and shall know that I am the LORD, when I have broken the bands of their yoke, and delivered them out of the hand of those that served themselves of them.

EZEKIEL 34:26–27

The earth and I have this in common—You care for our needs. Despite how we struggle in our pain—me counting the minutes to help them pass, and the earth groaning for redemption—even so, encircle us with Your goodness and help us meditate on the blessings You give.

....

....

....

....

....

....

....

....

....

....

....

....

My soul shall be satisfied as with marrow and fatness; and my mouth shall praise thee with joyful lips: when I remember thee upon my bed, and meditate on thee in the night watches.

Psalm 63:5–6

For the earth which drinketh in the rain that cometh oft upon it, and bringeth forth herbs meet for them by whom it is dressed, receiveth blessing from God.

Hebrews 6:7

People tell me that I am "blessed to be a blessing." How can I bless others when my life feels anything but "abounding in grace" right now, Father? But Your promise is there. Help me grasp Your boundless grace, ever praising You for the sufficiency You provide, so I can share Your blessing.

....

....

....

....

....

....

....

....

....

....

Blessed be the God and Father of our Lord Jesus Christ, who hath blessed us with all spiritual blessings in heavenly places in Christ.

EPHESIANS 1:3

And God is able to make all grace abound toward you; that ye, always having all sufficiency in all things, may abound to every good work: (As it is written, He hath dispersed abroad; he hath given to the poor: his righteousness remaineth for ever. Now he that ministereth seed to the sower both minister bread for your food, and multiply your seed sown, and increase the fruits of your righteousness;) Being enriched in every thing to all bountifulness, which causeth through us thanksgiving to God.

2 CORINTHIANS 9:8–11

Brokenheartedness

◆

Our emotions and our bodies are inextricably connected. Just as chronic pain can cause depression, heartbreak can initiate a downward spiral in our physical health. What has broken your heart? Sometimes the fallen world cracks us open, or others clumsily handle us when we're at our most vulnerable. We might ache, realizing how far we still have to go before we're healed. When we find ourselves in pieces, God is gentle with our shards; He is the skillful mender of broken hearts. Read these Bible promises, and be assured that your compassionate Creator loves you deeply, pieces and all.

He healeth the broken in heart,
and bindeth up their wounds.

PSALM 147:3

Loving Father, I feel betrayed—by my body, by my emotions. I don't know that I can take any more. But You call me to keep going, trusting that You will heal my heart. Bind up my wounds; help me to find solace in You who let Yourself be wounded for my sake.

....
....
....
....
....
....
....
....
....
....
....
....

My flesh and my heart faileth: but God is the strength of my heart, and my portion for ever.
PSALM 73:26

But do thou for me, O GOD the Lord, for thy name's sake: because thy mercy is good, deliver thou me. For I am poor and needy, and my heart is wounded within me.
PSALM 109:21–22

Creator God, thank You that You know me inside and out; You understand my heartbreak. Though now You collect my tears, give me hope in Your promise to restore me so I can lift my voice in praise to You, knowing that You are always near and ready to help.

....
....
....
....
....
....
....
....
....
....

O Lord, thou hast searched me, and known me. Thou knowest my downsitting and mine uprising, thou understandest my thought afar off. Thou compassest my path and my lying down, and art acquainted with all my ways. For there is not a word in my tongue, but, lo, O Lord, thou knowest it altogether.

Psalm 139:1–4

Thou tellest my wanderings: put thou my tears into thy bottle: are they not in thy book? . . . In God will I praise his word: in the Lord will I praise his word.

Psalm 56:8, 10

Comfort

———◆———

God isn't offended by our weeping or mourning—His heart is compassionate toward His children when they need comfort for their pain. Jesus gave us the Holy Spirit to be our Comforter. The Spirit prays for us when we have no words to speak for ourselves, and He guides us to the truth in the Word that we need at that moment. He can bring peace to our hearts through prayer and reading the Word even when the circumstances in our lives haven't changed yet. Read these Bible promises, and know that God never ignores our pleas for comfort.

Blessed be God, even the Father of our Lord Jesus Christ, the Father of mercies, and the God of all comfort; who comforteth us in all our tribulation, that we may be able to comfort them which are in any trouble, by the comfort wherewith we ourselves are comforted of God. For as the sufferings of Christ abound in us, so our consolation also aboundeth by Christ.

2 Corinthians 1:3–5

Nothing anyone says seems to help these days, Jesus. But You promise that everlasting comfort is found in You. Your love is tender as a mother's; You never turn away but instead strengthen Your people with grace and hope. I need Your comfort, Lord Jesus. . .let me feel it more than ever.

....

....

....

....

....

....

....

....

....

....

....

Now our Lord Jesus Christ himself, and God, even our Father, which hath loved us, and hath given us everlasting consolation and good hope through grace, comfort your hearts, and stablish you in every good word and work.

2 THESSALONIANS 2:16–17

As one whom his mother comforteth, so will I comfort you; and ye shall be comforted in Jerusalem.

ISAIAH 66:13

Your presence is a comfort, Emmanuel. Just as You were with David in the wilderness, You are with me in the doctor's office, the waiting room, the silent moments where I breathe through pain and long for wholeness. Through it all, help me remember that You are with me.

....

....

....

....

....

....

....

....

....

....

Yea, though I walk through the valley of the shadow of death, I will fear no evil: for thou art with me; thy rod and thy staff they comfort me.

PSALM 23:4

Lo, I am with you always, even unto the end of the world.

MATTHEW 28:20

My heart is heavy, Lord, but I am comforted when I lift
my voice in praise, to speak truth about Your promises.
My help comes from You, Mighty Maker of heaven
and earth. Though my troubles try to tell me otherwise,
remind me that I am safe in the circle of Your love.

....

....

....

....

....

....

....

....

....

....

*I will lift up mine eyes unto the hills, from whence cometh my help.
My help cometh from the LORD, which made heaven and earth. He
will not suffer thy foot to be moved: he that keepeth thee will not
slumber. Behold, he that keepeth Israel shall neither slumber nor sleep.
The LORD is thy keeper: the LORD is thy shade upon thy right hand.*

PSALM 121:1–5

*Thou hast turned for me my mourning into dancing:
thou hast put off my sackcloth, and girded me with gladness.*

PSALM 30:11

Community

When God created Eve, He demonstrated the necessity of community—"It is not good that the man should be alone" (Genesis 2:18). On our healing journey, we too need the loving support of a community. Not everyone will be a good fit, but God will provide those careful listeners, encouragers, and helpers we need to strengthen us. Whether we realize it or not, our community needs us too! We are a vital part of its life. Dwell on these Bible promises about the holy beauty of Christian fellowship—if you need a community, ask your heavenly Father, and He will provide.

Neither pray I for these alone, but for them also which shall believe on me through their word; that they all may be one; as thou, Father, art in me, and I in thee, that they also may be one in us: that the world may believe that thou hast sent me. And the glory which thou gavest me I have given them; that they may be one, even as we are one: I in them, and thou in me, that they may be made perfect in one; and that the world may know that thou hast sent me, and hast loved them, as thou hast loved me.

JOHN 17:20–23

Father, sometimes I feel like a broken record, bringing the same needs and prayer requests to my brothers and sisters. But You rejoice in Your children caring for one another, which reflects Your abundant love. Help me not draw back in shame or fear, but lean on the love of my community.

....

....

....

....

....

....

....

....

....

....

....

Two are better than one; because they have a good reward for their labour. For if they fall, the one will lift up his fellow: but woe to him that is alone when he falleth; for he hath not another to help him up. Again, if two lie together, then they have heat: but how can one be warm alone? And if one prevail against him, two shall withstand him; and a threefold cord is not quickly broken.

ECCLESIASTES 4:9–12

Bear ye one another's burdens, and so fulfil the law of Christ.

GALATIANS 6:2

Father, at times it feels like I am just being served by my church body and friends, but even in this season of healing, I can serve them too. Show me ways to love and serve my brothers and sisters as You do, that I may help build up Your holy saints.

....

....

....

....

....

....

....

....

....

....

This is my commandment, that ye love one another, as I have loved you. Greater love hath no man than this, that a man lay down his life for his friends.

JOHN 15:12–13

Let love be without dissimulation. Abhor that which is evil; cleave to that which is good. Be kindly affectioned one to another with brotherly love; in honour preferring one another; not slothful in business; fervent in spirit; serving the Lord; rejoicing in hope; patient in tribulation; continuing instant in prayer; distributing to the necessity of saints; given to hospitality.

ROMANS 12:9–13

Courage

◆

Courage doesn't mean that you are fearless. Instead, having courage means choosing to face the challenges before you and entrusting yourself—your fears and your efforts—to God. Maybe today's hurdle is getting out of bed for the first time in two days. Maybe it's finally making that phone call to ask for forgiveness. Perhaps it's yet another visit to the doctor that you've been dreading. Through everything, pray and ask to feel your Savior's presence go with you. Meditate on these Bible promises that proclaim that God's presence and strength can embolden us even in our most fearful moments.

Wait on the LORD: be of good courage, and he shall strengthen thine heart: wait, I say, on the LORD.

PSALM 27:14

Jesus, I remember the old hymn that says "Because He lives, I can face tomorrow." Because You live and are mightily at work, I can face *today*. Even if it's just one minute at a time. Dwell with me in that minute, that second—breathe grace into me, beautiful Savior.

....

....

....

♥ ....

....

....

....

....

....

....

....

....

These things I have spoken unto you, that in me ye might have peace. In the world ye shall have tribulation: but be of good cheer; I have overcome the world.

JOHN 16:33

Be of good courage, and he shall strengthen your heart, all ye that hope in the LORD.

PSALM 31:24

I don't think of myself as bold, not right now. But through You, my Deliverer, I can be! You are stronger than anything I come up against—*anything*. As I trust in You, give me boldness for the situations that leave me quaking— bold because You are always by my side.

For he hath said, I will never leave thee, nor forsake thee.
So that we may boldly say, The Lord is my helper,
and I will not fear what man shall do unto me.
HEBREWS 13:5–6

The wicked flee when no man pursueth:
but the righteous are bold as a lion.
PROVERBS 28:1

When darkness falls, when despair smothers and fear surrounds, strengthen that spirit of power You gave me, Father. Let Your love blaze through my veins, and fill my mind with the truth of Your Word. With You holding me up, I can be brave, for You are my righteous God who helps me.

....
....
....
....
....
....
....
....
....
....
....
....

For God hath not given us the spirit of fear;
but of power, and of love, and of a sound mind.

2 TIMOTHY 1:7

Fear thou not; for I am with thee: be not dismayed; for I am
thy God: I will strengthen thee; yea, I will help thee; yea,
I will uphold thee with the right hand of my righteousness.

ISAIAH 41:10

Depending on God

---◆---

Though certainty in life is an illusion, we love it all the same—and we miss it terribly when we're hit with the unexpected. There are no certainties in illness and recovery, just plans, probabilities, and "best results." God is our Rock and our Strong Deliverer during uncertainty. Though He doesn't always reveal what's coming next for us, we know He is unchangeable in His love, wisdom, and strength to help. In these Bible promises, the Word speaks with certainty that God blesses those who trust in His mercy, seek His wisdom, and draw their life from Him.

But let all those that put their trust in thee rejoice:
let them ever shout for joy, because thou defendest them:
let them also that love thy name be joyful in thee.

PSALM 5:11

God, I struggle to see Your good plans while I'm in the middle of this journey. Though nothing else is certain, I know You are—Your faithfulness and goodness don't change. Help me trust Your sustaining love today, Father; hold me up, take my burden—I cannot carry it alone.

....
....
....
....
....
....
....
....
....
....
....
....

Cast thy burden upon the LORD, and he shall sustain thee:
he shall never suffer the righteous to be moved.

PSALM 55:22

The fear of man bringeth a snare: but whoso
putteth his trust in the LORD shall be safe.

PROVERBS 29:25

Lord, right now depending on You feels less like resting peacefully and more like grabbing fistfuls of Your robe and just barely hanging on. But by Your grace, I am still holding on. I long for healing, to see You work mightily in my life. Help me keep following hard after You.

....
....
....
....
....
....
....
....
....
....
....
....

For the Lord GOD will help me; therefore shall I not be confounded: therefore have I set my face like a flint, and I know that I shall not be ashamed.

ISAIAH 50:7

Because thou hast been my help, therefore in the shadow of thy wings will I rejoice. My soul followeth hard after thee: thy right hand upholdeth me.

PSALM 63:7–8

Depression

◆

Many faithful men and women in scripture dealt with the despondency and intense sadness of depression. They cried out to God, and He answered them in their emotional, physical, and spiritual need. Today, we are blessed with information about many kinds of depression, as well as health professionals and counselors whom God has gifted with the skills to help and heal. As you explore the options to best care for yourself, read these Bible promises and remember that God loves you beyond measure. He's near to you in your pain, and His gentle strength will guide and lift you up.

Through the tender mercy of our God; whereby the dayspring from on high hath visited us, to give light to them that sit in darkness and in the shadow of death, to guide our feet into the way of peace.

LUKE 1:78–79

How long will I be there, Lord? The days crawl. Where is the good You promise? These feelings hurt and are ugly, but I know You want to hear it all. I'm stuck in the valley; I need to know You are still there watching over me. Show me I am not alone.

....

....

....

....

....

....

....

....

....

....

....

My heart is smitten, and withered like grass; so that I forget to eat my bread. By reason of the voice of my groaning my bones cleave to my skin. . . . I watch, and am as a sparrow alone upon the house top. . . . But thou, O LORD, shall endure for ever; and thy remembrance unto all generations. Thou shalt arise, and have mercy upon Zion: for the time to favour her, yea, the set time, is come.

PSALM 102:4–5, 7, 12–13

Trust in him at all times; ye people, pour out your heart before him: God is a refuge for us. Selah.

PSALM 62:8

Jesus, I move toward You, for where else will I find help? You say that You will rescue me; show me! Hold me close when I have no strength left to cling to You; restore the joy of my salvation—let Your light come breaking in upon me.

....

....

....

....

....

....

....

....

....

....

....

Therefore I will look unto the LORD; I will wait for the God of my salvation: my God will hear me. Rejoice not against me, O mine enemy: when I fall, I shall arise; when I sit in darkness, the LORD shall be a light unto me.

MICAH 7:7–8

Why art thou cast down, O my soul? and why art thou disquieted within me? hope thou in God: for I shall yet praise him, who is the health of my countenance, and my God.

PSALM 42:11

Lord God, on You I wait, trusting You are who You say: loving, mighty to save, ever faithful. Though this night is long and the enemy's lies pound away at me, I will keep my heart set on Your promise to rescue me, gracious Father, and fill my mouth with praise.

....
....
....
....
....
....
....
....
....
....
....

*The LORD upholdeth all that fall, and raiseth
up all those that be bowed down.*

PSALM 145:14

*I waited patiently for the LORD; and he inclined unto me, and heard
my cry. He brought me up also out of an horrible pit, out of the miry
clay, and set my feet upon a rock, and established my goings. And he
hath put a new song in my mouth, even praise unto our God:
many shall see it, and fear, and shall trust in the LORD.*

PSALM 40:1–3

Encouragement

*D*uring the healing process, we are especially vulnerable to worry and despair. When the light of hope in our hearts fades to a flicker, the Holy Spirit sends encouragement to fan the flame. He communicates God's truth and love to us through other believers, prayer, and our time in the Word. Sometimes He sends encouragement when we least expect it—a hilarious joke or an empathetic stranger at the grocery store. We too can share the encouragement He's given us! Read these Bible promises about the power of encouragement—God can enliven your heart even on its most trying days.

Heaviness in the heart of man maketh it stoop: but a good word maketh it glad.

PROVERBS 12:25

Jesus, thank You for the Bible, that I'm able to read about Your words and miracles when You walked on earth and also revisit the vibrant stories of my brothers and sisters in the faith. They struggled too, but You upheld them. Lead me to the encouragement I need today.

....

....

....

....

....

....

....

....

....

....

....

For whatsoever things were written aforetime were written for our learning, that we through patience and comfort of the scriptures might have hope.

ROMANS 15:4

But be filled with the Spirit; speaking to yourselves in psalms and hymns and spiritual songs, singing and making melody in your heart to the Lord; giving thanks always for all things unto God and the Father in the name of our Lord Jesus Christ.

EPHESIANS 5:18–20

Breathe new life into my tired soul, Lord. You who
created everything and hold it all together—fire up my heart
so I can praise Your name. Let Your truth enliven me today;
send it how You will—through dear Christian friends,
Your Word, or Your Spirit's nudges in prayer.

....
....
....
....
....
....
....
....
....
....
....
....

*The LORD is my strength and song, and is become my salvation.
The voice of rejoicing and salvation is in the tabernacles of
the righteous: the right hand of the LORD doeth valiantly.*

PSALM 118:14–15

*For whatsoever is born of God overcometh the world: and this is the
victory that overcometh the world, even our faith. Who is he that
overcometh the world, but he that believeth that Jesus is the Son of God?*

I JOHN 5:4–5

Eternity

◆

As God's people, we are pilgrims on this earth, serving faithfully as we look forward to our true home in heaven with Christ. The hope of eternity is even sweeter for those of us who suffer bodily now, because we know that no matter the severity of our condition, we will be completely healed in Jesus' presence. He has promised to make all things—and us—new! Hold on to these Bible promises when the present hurt grows too heavy to bear—eternity has no more tears or pain, and we will live forever in the light of our beautiful Savior.

And I heard a great voice out of heaven saying, Behold, the tabernacle of God is with men, and he will dwell with them, and they shall be his people, and God himself shall be with them, and be their God. And God shall wipe away all tears from their eyes; and there shall be no more death, neither sorrow, nor crying, neither shall there be any more pain: for the former things are passed away.

REVELATION 21:3–4

Nothing and no one can take Your gift of heaven from me, Lord. Thank You for Your promise! This pain, though constant, is fleeting compared to the time I will spend with You. But I am still in the here and now; strengthen and guide me until we meet face to face.

....
....
....
....
....
....
....
....
....
....
....

Thou shalt guide me with thy counsel,
and afterward receive me to glory.
PSALM 73:24

And this is the Father's will which hath sent me, that of all
which he hath given me I should lose nothing, but should raise it
up again at the last day. And this is the will of him that sent me,
that every one which seeth the Son, and believeth on him, may
have everlasting life: and I will raise him up at the last day.
JOHN 6:39–40

Jesus, there are days I just want to be with You, to go to the home You've prepared for Your people. But I'm here, still hurting, still moving forward. With my eyes on heaven, help me focus my heart on trusting You. I'm thankful that You are near now and forever.

....

....

....

....

....

....

....

....

....

....

....

*Then shall the King say unto them on his right hand,
Come, ye blessed of my Father, inherit the kingdom
prepared for you from the foundation of the world.*

MATTHEW 25:34

*In my Father's house are many mansions: if it were not so,
I would have told you. I go to prepare a place for you. And if
I go and prepare a place for you, I will come again, and receive
you unto myself; that where I am, there ye may be also.*

JOHN 14:2–3

Jesus, thank You for the promise of restoration in heaven, where pain is forever banished and Your people are free from sin. But You are already at work now shaping me to be like You. The process is hard. . .but I will trust in Your love till Your work is complete.

....
....
....
....
....
....
....
....
....
....
....

Beloved, now are we the sons of God, and it doth not yet appear what we shall be: but we know that, when he shall appear, we shall be like him; for we shall see him as he is.

1 JOHN 3:2

And there shall be no more curse: but the throne of God and of the Lamb shall be in it; and his servants shall serve him: and they shall see his face; and his name shall be in their foreheads. And there shall be no night there; and they need no candle, neither light of the sun; for the Lord God giveth them light: and they shall reign for ever and ever.

REVELATION 22:3–5

Faith

◆

$\mathcal{F}$aith is being confident of God's promises even when we can't see when they'll be fulfilled. Maybe someone's told you, "If you had more faith, you'd be healed." God isn't waiting for us to "believe enough"; He wants us to put our faith in His power and His good plan for us, not in how much we believe. Just like the saints of old, we can trust our faithful God to sustain us without us knowing all the details. Read these Bible promises, and see how God strengthens our hearts to trust His good plan even during our hardest journeys.

But with the precious blood of Christ, as of a lamb without blemish and without spot:. . .who by him do believe in God, that raised him up from the dead, and gave him glory; that your faith and hope might be in God.

1 PETER 1:19, 21

Faithful One, Your Word tells me that You reward those who seek You. I can't see ahead to what Your plans are, but I will live by faith, live on faith—for You are worthy of trust. You know what worries me today, so strengthen my faith to stay on You.

....
....
....
....
....
....
....
....
....
....
....
....
....

*But without faith it is impossible to please him: for he
that cometh to God must believe that he is, and that
he is a rewarder of them that diligently seek him.*

HEBREWS 11:6

*For therein is the righteousness of God revealed from
faith to faith: as it is written, The just shall live by faith.*

ROMANS 1:17

You tell me my faith is more precious than gold to You, Lord. My healing journey is an opportunity for my faith to grow, to be refined—but the weight of the trial hangs heavy on me. Yet Your grace is near. Help me stay connected to You in prayer through it all.

....

....

....

....

....

....

....

....

....

Wherein ye greatly rejoice, though now for a season, if need be, ye are in heaviness through manifold temptations: that the trial of your faith, being much more precious than of gold that perisheth, though it be tried with fire, might be found unto praise and honour and glory at the appearing of Jesus Christ.

1 PETER 1:6–7

Jesus answered and said unto them, Verily I say unto you, If ye have faith, and doubt not, ye shall not only do this which is done to the fig tree, but also if ye shall say unto this mountain, Be thou removed, and be thou cast into the sea; it shall be done. And all things, whatsoever ye shall ask in prayer, believing, ye shall receive.

MATTHEW 21:21–22

Forgiveness

$\mathscr{A}$s we walk through life, God's forgiveness is a precious assurance. We can stand boldly in His presence, knowing that Jesus has already paid for our every sin and shame. Because He has so generously covered our sins with love, God calls us to reflect Him by forgiving those who have wronged us. Depending on the offense, we may have to bring our hurt to the Father again and again, asking for His strength and compassion to forgive. These Bible promises show that we can be confident in God's forgiveness and that He will help us extend forgiveness to others.

Who is a God like unto thee, that pardoneth iniquity, and passeth by the transgression of the remnant of his heritage? He retaineth not his anger for ever, because he delighteth in mercy. He will turn again, he will have compassion upon us; he will subdue our iniquities; and thou wilt cast all their sins into the depths of the sea.

MICAH 7:18–19

Father God, because You are loving and merciful, You sent Your Son to rescue sin-bound humanity from their chains. There is no exhausting Your mercy, Your love for those who repent! When I tremble to bring my offenses before You, remind me of Your mercy, that You are eager to forgive.

....

....

....

....

....

....

....

....

....

....

....

....

He hath not dealt with us after our sins; nor rewarded us according to our iniquities. For as the heaven is high above the earth, so great is his mercy toward them that fear him. As far as the east is from the west, so far hath he removed our transgressions from us.

PSALM 103:10–12

For I will be merciful to their unrighteousness, and their sins and their iniquities will I remember no more.

HEBREWS 8:12

Jesus, Your forgiveness is such a beautiful gift! No matter what it is or how many times I've struggled, when I confess, You take the burden off my shoulders; the sin I carried is gone. Thank You for inviting me to confess, and for promising that I will always find forgiveness in You.

....

....

....

....

....

....

....

....

....

....

....

....

Blessed is he whose transgression is forgiven, whose sin is covered. Blessed is the man unto whom the LORD imputeth not iniquity, and in whose spirit there is no guile.

PSALM 32:1–2

If we confess our sins, he is faithful and just to forgive us our sins, and to cleanse us from all unrighteousness.

1 JOHN 1:9

Lord, You know the people I struggle to forgive. It feels impossible to let go of how they've hurt me. But in Christ You forgave me for everything I've done, and You call Your children to follow Your example. Help me forgive them, Lord—as many times as it takes.

....

....

....

....

....

....

....

....

....

....

....

....

Forbearing one another, and forgiving one another, if any man have a quarrel against any: even as Christ forgave you, so also do ye.

COLOSSIANS 3:13

Let all bitterness, and wrath, and anger, and clamour, and evil speaking, be put away from you, with all malice: and be ye kind one to another, tenderhearted, forgiving one another, even as God for Christ's sake hath forgiven you.

EPHESIANS 4:31–32

Frustration

"Are You listening, God? I just can't handle this anymore!" We can get so frustrated with where we are physically or spiritually. It doesn't help matters when we deal with uncompassionate doctors, patronizing family members, or difficult side effects of medication. Many heroes of the Bible also felt this bone-deep frustration. Yet in the midst of venting their pain and fear to God, they also held on to their belief in His goodness. Read these groups of verses that show examples of God's people crying out to Him in frustration and how their hearts found comfort in His powerful promises.

I am feeble and sore broken: I have roared by reason of the disquietness of my heart. Lord, all my desire is before thee; and my groaning is not hid from thee. My heart panteth, my strength faileth me: as for the light of mine eyes, it also is gone from me. . . . For in thee, O LORD, do I hope: thou wilt hear, O Lord my God.

PSALM 38:8–10, 15

I want to pray as Jeremiah did, Father, to be honest about my feelings, to pour out my frustration, knowing that You hear "the voice of my weeping." Let Your truth sink down into my wounds, physical and spiritual, soothing them with the balm of the promise that You will help me.

....

....

....

....

....

....

....

....

Why is my pain perpetual, and my wound incurable, which refuseth to be healed? wilt thou be altogether unto me as a liar, and as waters that fail? . . . And they shall fight against thee, but they shall not prevail against thee: for I am with thee to save thee and to deliver thee, saith the LORD. And I will deliver thee out of the hand of the wicked, and I will redeem thee out of the hand of the terrible.

JEREMIAH 15:18, 20–21

Have mercy upon me, O LORD; for I am weak: O LORD, heal me; for my bones are vexed. My soul is also sore vexed: but thou, O LORD, how long? . . . Depart from me, all ye workers of iniquity; for the LORD hath heard the voice of my weeping. The LORD hath heard my supplication; the LORD will receive my prayer.

PSALM 6:2–3, 8–9

Though I am frustrated with others, with my pain, with my slow healing journey, I turn my mind to remember this truth: You have not forgotten me. I will dwell on Your grace, the works of Your hands; You in Your goodness will quench the thirst for freedom, for healing, in my spirit.

....

....

....

....

....

....

....

....

....

....

Hath God forgotten to be gracious? hath he in anger shut up his tender mercies? Selah. And I said, This is my infirmity: but I will remember the years of the right hand of the most High. I will remember the works of the LORD: surely I will remember thy wonders of old.

PSALM 77:9–11

Therefore is my spirit overwhelmed within me; my heart within me is desolate. I remember the days of old; I meditate on all thy works; I muse on the work of thy hands. I stretch forth my hands unto thee: my soul thirsteth after thee, as a thirsty land. Selah.

PSALM 143:4–6

God Is in Control

Our heavenly Father is the sovereign King over all creation, so nothing can happen outside of His will. He sometimes allows difficult things to enter our lives, and though we wrestle with them, we know that nothing happens to us "by accident." God has a purpose for everything, and He works out everything for good to those who love Him. The Holy Spirit comforts and guides our hearts, helping us to continue trusting in God's loving sovereignty. Take courage from these Bible promises that attest that He reigns over all, down to the smallest details of our lives.

And we know that all things work together for good to them that love God, to them who are the called according to his purpose.

ROMANS 8:28

Father, help me look for the good that You are working in my life and others' lives through my healing journey. I am comforted reading about how although the blind man in John endured decades of blindness, You used his life for Your glory. Let Your glory shine through me too, Lord.

....

....

....

....

....

....

....

....

....

And as Jesus passed by, he saw a man which was blind from his birth. And his disciples asked him, saying, Master, who did sin, this man, or his parents, that he was born blind? Jesus answered, Neither hath this man sinned, nor his parents: but that the works of God should be made manifest in him. . . . When he had thus spoken, he spat on the ground, and made clay of the spittle, and he anointed the eyes of the blind man with the clay, and said unto him, Go, wash in the pool of Siloam, (which is by interpretation, Sent.) He went his way therefore, and washed, and came seeing.

JOHN 9:1–3, 6–7

But Jesus beheld them, and said unto them, With men this is impossible; but with God all things are possible.

MATTHEW 19:26

Father, I know my strength is nothing compared to Yours, my wisdom only foolishness, but I struggle to let go of controlling my life—or what I think is control. But You reign over all things in justice and in truth—help me submit my path to You, my good and loving God.

....

....

....

....

....

....

....

....

....

....

....

....

....

....

....

A man's heart deviseth his way:
but the LORD directeth his steps.

PROVERBS 16:9

For the word of the LORD is right;
and all his works are done in truth.

PSALM 33:4

How great You are, Lord! I praise You for Your trustworthy character. Because Your heart is compassionate, You will not let Your children languish without help. But when I can't see the way, hold my hand in the darkness—Your hand, powerful and mighty, is gentle too—and be my light.

....

....

....

....

....

....

....

....

....

....

Thine, O LORD is the greatness, and the power, and the glory, and the victory, and the majesty: for all that is in the heaven and in the earth is thine; thine is the kingdom, O LORD, and thou art exalted as head above all. Both riches and honour come of thee, and thou reignest over all; and in thine hand is power and might; and in thine hand it is to make great, and to give strength unto all.

1 CHRONICLES 29:11–12

The LORD shall preserve thee from all evil: he shall preserve thy soul. The LORD shall preserve thy going out and thy coming in from this time forth, and even for evermore.

PSALM 121:7–8

God's Goodness

---◆---

When we see or experience suffering, it's not unusual for us to question our Creator. "Aren't You good? Then why is this happening?" We must turn to the truth of the Word to realign our heart's vision. We daily experience the effects of a world mired in sin, and scripture testifies that God's people will suffer hardship in this life too. However, the Word also proclaims that God shows His eternal goodness, mercy, and strength toward all He loves! Meditate on these Bible promises that reveal His character, and reflect on how His goodness is present in your life.

Oh how great is thy goodness, which thou hast laid up
for them that fear thee; which thou hast wrought for
them that trust in thee before the sons of men!

Psalm 31:19

God, I am amazed to think that the earth is intimately
acquainted with Your goodness, even full to bursting with it!
Pain can cloud my view of Your goodness, but open my eyes,
Father; surprise me with its abundance. I know You can
teach me to know and do good as You do.

....

....

....

....

....

....

....

....

....

He loveth righteousness and judgment:
the earth is full of the goodness of the LORD.
PSALM 33:5

The earth, O LORD, is full of thy mercy: teach me thy statutes. Thou
hast dealt well with thy servant, O LORD, according unto thy word.
Teach me good judgment and knowledge: for I have believed thy
commandments. Before I was afflicted I went astray: but now have I
kept thy word. Thou art good, and doest good; teach me thy statutes.
PSALM 119:64–68

Jesus, even in the midst of everything I walk through now,
I set my hope on Your promise: Your goodness protects me,
Your goodness can and will fill my empty places, You will
satisfy me and never turn me away. Feed my hungry soul,
Savior, and fill my mouth with praise!

....

....

....

....

....

....

....

....

....

....

....

....

....

*The LORD is good, a strong hold in the day of trouble;
and he knoweth them that trust in him.*

NAHUM 1:7

*Oh that men would praise the LORD for his goodness, and for
his wonderful works to the children of men! For he satisfieth
the longing soul, and filleth the hungry soul with goodness.*

PSALM 107:8–9

God's Love

---◆---

It is so important to remember how much our Creator loves us, because it can be so hard for us to be kind to ourselves when we're hurting. We see our flaws, our shameful secrets, our failures. But God didn't lavish His love on us because we'd earned it. When we had no interest in loving Him, He demonstrated His love by sending Jesus to save us. God's powerful love animates our souls from death to abundant life in Christ. He loves you now and always will, no matter what. Soak up these Bible promises that demonstrate His unchanging love!

In this was manifested the love of God toward us, because that God sent his only begotten Son into the world, that we might live through him. Herein is love, not that we loved God, but that he loved us, and sent his Son to be the propitiation for our sins.

1 JOHN 4:9–10

Father, to You I sing, "Could we with ink the ocean fill, and were the skies of parchment made, were every stalk on earth a quill. . .to write the love of God above would drain the ocean dry; nor could the scroll contain the whole, though stretched from sky to sky" ("The Love of God," Frederick M. Lehman. Public Domain.).

....

....

....

....

....

....

....

....

....

....

That ye, being rooted and grounded in love, may be able to comprehend with all saints what is the breadth, and length, and depth, and height; and to know the love of Christ, which passeth knowledge, that ye might be filled with all the fulness of God.

Ephesians 3:17–19

For I am persuaded, that neither death, nor life, nor angels, nor principalities, nor powers, nor things present, nor things to come, nor height, nor depth, nor any other creature, shall be able to separate us from the love of God, which is in Christ Jesus our Lord.

Romans 8:38–39

Thank You, Jesus, for loving us so much You gave Yourself to save us. Your love transforms my heart, teaching me to follow You and to love others! I set my hope on You—in this healing journey Your love will sustain me, and my life is hidden in You.

....

....

....

....

....

....

....

....

....

....

....

....

....

I am crucified with Christ: nevertheless I live; yet not I, but Christ liveth in me: and the life which I now live in the flesh I live by the faith of the Son of God, who loved me, and gave himself for me.

GALATIANS 2:20

And walk in love, as Christ also hath loved us, and hath given himself for us an offering and a sacrifice to God for a sweetsmelling savour.

EPHESIANS 5:2

Lord Jesus, weak and weary, I reach out to grab ahold of You and the full joy You offer. When I have trouble believing the great love You have for me, teach me to abide, to soak in Your song and Your love that restores, heals, and strengthens Your people.

....
....
....
....
....
....
....
....
....
....
....
....

As the Father hath loved me, so have I loved you: continue ye in my love. If ye keep my commandments, ye shall abide in my love; even as I have kept my Father's commandments, and abide in his love. These things have I spoken unto you, that my joy might remain in you, and that your joy might be full.

JOHN 15:9–11

The LORD thy God in the midst of thee is mighty; he will save, he will rejoice over thee with joy; he will rest in his love, he will joy over thee with singing.

ZEPHANIAH 3:17

God's Plan for Me

When we're seeking healing, we're bombarded on all sides with "plans"—initial treatments, then backup strategies in case the previous ones fail. We may make our own private plans—"I want to be better by Christmas"—and then get discouraged if our recovery doesn't follow our hoped-for timetable. It can be so difficult to see what step to take next, let alone imagine the finish line. Thankfully, in uncertainty we still have hope in the Almighty. These Bible promises show that God has a redemptive plan for our lives— He will guide your steps as you trust in Him.

The steps of a good man are ordered by the LORD:
and he delighteth in his way. Though he fall,
he shall not be utterly cast down: for the
LORD upholdeth him with his hand.

PSALM 37:23–24

Lord, I am thankful You know the arc of my journey, that You will use my life to Your glory. But today it's hard. I just want more certainty about what You are doing. Give me grace; guide me in Your truth. Help me trust You to accomplish Your good purpose!

....

....

....

....

....

....

....

....

....

....

....

In whom also we have obtained an inheritance, being predestinated according to the purpose of him who worketh all things after the counsel of his own will: that we should be to the praise of his glory, who first trusted in Christ.

EPHESIANS 1:11–12

For since the beginning of the world men have not heard, nor perceived by the ear, neither hath the eye seen, O God, beside thee, what he hath prepared for him that waiteth for him.

ISAIAH 64:4

Father, though I don't know how long my healing journey will be, there is part of Your plan I do know: You have created good works for me to walk in. While my limitations are still here, guide me to see Your provision so I can serve You with all I have.

....

....

....

....

....

....

....

....

....

....

....

....

....

For we are his workmanship, created in Christ Jesus unto good works, which God hath before ordained that we should walk in them.
EPHESIANS 2:10

I will instruct thee and teach thee in the way which thou shalt go: I will guide thee with mine eye.
PSALM 32:8

God's Power

---◆---

The Creator that set the stars in place and filled the deepest oceans knows our names and our struggles. The same power that raised Jesus from the grave is working in the lives of all of us who believe in Him. He renews us daily, strengthening us to follow Christ faithfully in all circumstances. Nothing is impossible with God; He will bring restoration and beauty out of our pain, even if we don't receive complete healing in this life. If you feel powerless, reflect on these Bible promises about how you have access to God's infinite, loving power through Christ.

The LORD reigneth, he is clothed with majesty; the LORD is clothed with strength, wherewith he hath girded himself: the world also is stablished, that it cannot be moved.

PSALM 93:1

I need Your strength today, Lord: to have that hard conversation, to undergo surgery, to stand strong against the enemy's lies. But You are my Rock, strong and mighty; You prepare me for what lies ahead. With You I can do things I never thought possible! Empower me today, Lord.

....

....

....

....

....

....

....

....

....

....

....

....

For who is God save the LORD? or who is a rock save our God? It is God that girdeth me with strength, and maketh my way perfect. He maketh my feet like hinds' feet, and setteth me upon my high places.

PSALM 18:31–33

For though he was crucified through weakness, yet he liveth by the power of God. For we also are weak in him, but we shall live with him by the power of God toward you.

2 CORINTHIANS 13:4

God, You are powerful to accomplish all of Your good plan. Though I don't know what my healing will look like in the next bit of the journey, I know You can accomplish it, and I trust in Your love toward me. Remind me to keep asking, to keep trusting You.

....

....

....

....

....

....

....

....

....

....

And what is the exceeding greatness of his power to us-ward who believe, according to the working of his mighty power, which he wrought in Christ, when he raised him from the dead, and set him at his own right hand in the heavenly places, far above all principality, and power, and might, and dominion, and every name that is named, not only in this world, but also in that which is to come.

EPHESIANS 1:19–21

Now unto him that is able to do exceeding abundantly above all that we ask or think, according to the power that worketh in us, unto him be glory in the church by Christ Jesus throughout all ages, world without end. Amen.

EPHESIANS 3:20–21

Jesus, Your Word says that all things hold together because
of You—I can barely wrap my mind around this—but
You also told Your disciples that peace is found in You,
that You hold us together in this world. I am humbled—
remind me of Your power when I long for peace.

....

....

....

....

....

....

....

....

....

....

*For by him were all things created, that are in heaven, and that
are in earth, visible and invisible, whether they be thrones, or
dominions, or principalities, or powers: all things were created by him,
and for him: and he is before all things, and by him all things consist.*

COLOSSIANS 1:16–17

*These things I have spoken unto you, that in me ye might
have peace. In the world ye shall have tribulation:
but be of good cheer; I have overcome the world.*

JOHN 16:33

Gratitude

Gratitude takes practice, especially during trials. But having a thankful attitude is more than just "the right thing to do"—it's a powerful agent for hope and healing too. Through gratitude, we choose to embrace God's blessings over focusing on the hard things, and our hearts remain soft toward Him. Practicing thankfulness can also help us be more confident in prayer; after naming God's faithful work we've seen in our lives, we're assured of His goodness and can bravely ask Him to show us more. These Bible promises show that God's people are blessed when their hearts overflow with thanksgiving.

Make a joyful noise unto the LORD, all ye lands.
Serve the LORD with gladness: come before his
presence with singing. Know ye that the LORD he is
God: it is he that hath made us, and not we ourselves;
we are his people, and the sheep of his pasture. Enter
into his gates with thanksgiving, and into his courts
with praise: be thankful unto him, and bless his name.
For the LORD is good; his mercy is everlasting;
and his truth endureth to all generations.

PSALM 100:1–5

Father, Your Word instructs me to do everything with a thankful heart. So that means giving thanks inside the PET scan machine, puffing out thanks during physical therapy exercises, sighing my thanks while paying the bills? Teach my heart to reach for thanks first instead of grumbling, no matter what the day holds.

....

....

....

....

....

....

....

....

....

....

....

And whatsoever ye do in word or deed, do all in the name of the Lord Jesus, giving thanks to God and the Father by him.
COLOSSIANS 3:17

Although the fig tree shall not blossom, neither shall fruit be in the vines; the labour of the olive shall fail, and the fields shall yield no meat; the flock shall be cut off from the fold, and there shall be no herd in the stalls: yet I will rejoice in the Lord, I will joy in the God of my salvation.
HABAKKUK 3:17–18

Today I'll try to list the reasons I have to be grateful, though I know I will definitely run out of room before I've exhausted Your blessings. How amazing! But on days when pain or struggle makes my list feel short, show me anew Your love and faithfulness, and I'll praise You for them.

....

....

....

....

....

....

....

....

....

....

....

....

It is a good thing to give thanks unto the LORD, and to sing praises unto thy name, O Most High: to shew forth thy lovingkindness in the morning, and thy faithfulness every night. . . . For thou, LORD, hast made me glad through thy work: I will triumph in the works of thy hands.

PSALM 92:1–2, 4

By him therefore let us offer the sacrifice of praise to God continually, that is, the fruit of our lips giving thanks to his name.

HEBREWS 13:15

Grief

———◆———

*L*oss is one of the most painful experiences we can undergo in this life. We grieve for our loved ones who have died. We grieve for the abilities and activities that illness has taken from us. We weep for irreparable relationships. Loss hurts so much because creation wasn't meant to experience it—the Fall gave birth to death and sorrow. Jesus conquered death at the cross, but He too was touched by grief during His earthly life. These Bible promises remind us that Jesus understands our heart's deepest sorrow, and He will stay near us to give us comfort and hope.

Blessed are they that mourn:
for they shall be comforted.
MATTHEW 5:4

The reminders come daily, Father. Dear friends tell me
that grief will be like a stormy sea—some days the waves
mount high and crash over me, on others the water will
seem calmer. When my grief washes over my head, Lord,
hold me up by Your grace. . .keep me afloat.

....
....
....
....
....
....
....
....
....
....

In God is my salvation and my glory: the rock of my strength,
and my refuge, is in God. Trust in him at all times; ye people,
pour out your heart before him: God is a refuge for us. Selah.
PSALM 62:7–8

Thy righteousness also, O God, is very high, who hast done great
things: O God, who is like unto thee! Thou, which hast shewed me
great and sore troubles, shalt quicken me again, and shalt bring
me up again from the depths of the earth. Thou shalt increase
my greatness, and comfort me on every side.
PSALM 71:19–21

Father, so much will never be the same again for me. It hurts so much to think of it; my heart aches. Thank You for Your promise to be near, to restore me, to see You face to face one day—but help me bear this now. Comfort me by Your Spirit.

....

....

....

....

....

....

....

....

....

....

....

....

The LORD is nigh unto them that are of a broken heart; and saveth such as be of a contrite spirit. Many are the afflictions of the righteous: but the LORD delivereth him out of them all.

PSALM 34:18–19

And God shall wipe away all tears from their eyes; and there shall be no more death, neither sorrow, nor crying, neither shall there be any more pain: for the former things are passed away.

REVELATION 21:4

Jesus, as I grieve, You understand—You, the Man of Sorrows who bore such great grief to bring us the victory, to give us hope. Bolster my heart with the truth that You are close, that Your comfort can cover even this heart-wound of mine. Fill me with Your peace, Lord Jesus.

....

....

....

....

....

....

....

....

....

....

So when this corruptible shall have put on incorruption, and this mortal shall have put on immortality, then shall be brought to pass the saying that is written, Death is swallowed up in victory. O death, where is thy sting? O grave, where is thy victory? The sting of death is sin; and the strength of sin is the law. But thanks be to God, which giveth us the victory through our Lord Jesus Christ.

1 CORINTHIANS 15:54–57

For the LORD shall comfort Zion: he will comfort all her waste places; and he will make her wilderness like Eden, and her desert like the garden of the LORD; joy and gladness shall be found therein, thanksgiving, and the voice of melody.

ISAIAH 51:3

Healing

We see miraculous healing in story after story in scripture. Jesus cast out demons, opened the eyes of the blind, cured leprosy, and raised the dead to life again. As we read, we're encouraged not just by Jesus' miraculous power but by what those healings signified—that He would heal us from our sins and restore our relationship with God. Just as we entrust our salvation to Him, we trust Him to heal our earthly bodies according to the Father's will. These Bible promises show that our compassionate Savior draws near to comfort, heal, and restore us.

Bless the LORD, O my soul, and forget not all his benefits: who forgiveth all thine iniquities; who healeth all thy diseases.

PSALM 103:2–3

Jesus, I am thankful for Your miracles in the Word! Your power is perfect, not to be undone or overcome by the brokenness of this world. This healing journey has been so long—but I trust Your compassion and Your love for me. Help me to keep trusting in You.

....

....

....

....

....

....

....

....

When the even was come, they brought unto him many that were possessed with devils: and he cast out the spirits with his word, and healed all that were sick: that it might be fulfilled which was spoken by Esaias the prophet, saying, Himself took our infirmities, and bare our sicknesses.

MATTHEW 8:16–17

The Spirit of the Lord GOD is upon me; because the LORD hath anointed me to preach good tidings unto the meek; he hath sent me to bind up the brokenhearted, to proclaim liberty to the captives, and the opening of the prison to them that are bound; to proclaim the acceptable year of the LORD, and the day of vengeance of our God; to comfort all that mourn.

ISAIAH 61:1–2

Dear Jesus, You are my Good Shepherd—You care for all the members of Your flock, and that means me too. Today carry me close to Your heart, bind up my wounds, fill my hungry soul, and however long the healing process takes, let me never take my eyes off You.

....

....

....

....

....

....

....

....

....

....

....

I will feed my flock, and I will cause them to lie down, saith the Lord GOD. I will seek that which was lost, and bring again that which was driven away, and will bind up that which was broken, and will strengthen that which was sick.

EZEKIEL 34:15–16

Then they cry unto the LORD in their trouble, and he saveth them out of their distresses. He sent his word, and healed them, and delivered them from their destructions.

PSALM 107:19–20

Hope

*H*ope is more than a wish that things will turn out okay; it is living boldly with bravery and confidence. Hope stares down desperate situations and stands firm on God's promises—His faithfulness, His nearness, and His everlasting love and care for His children. On our healing journeys, it's essential for us to hold on to Christ and His promise that He will work all things out for our good. We don't have to wish that things are going to be okay; we *know* they will be. Reflect on these Bible promises that show how hope anchors us in tumultuous times.

Wherein God, willing more abundantly to shew unto the heirs of promise the immutability of his counsel, confirmed it by an oath: that by two immutable things, in which it was impossible for God to lie, we might have a strong consolation, who have fled for refuge to lay hold upon the hope set before us: which hope we have as an anchor of the soul, both sure and stedfast, and which entereth into that within the veil; whither the forerunner is for us entered, even Jesus, made an high priest for ever after the order of Melchisedec.

HEBREWS 6:17–20

Father, it's easy to place my hope in earthly things I can see and touch; I can write plans, take my medicines, attend my appointments. But You are my true and living hope—the One who will not fail me. Let me always set my expectation on You.

....

....

....

....

....

....

....

....

....

....

....

....

Blessed is the man that trusteth in the LORD, and whose hope the LORD is. For he shall be as a tree planted by the waters, and that spreadeth out her roots by the river, and shall not see when heat cometh, but her leaf shall be green; and shall not be careful in the year of drought, neither shall cease from yielding fruit.

JEREMIAH 17:7–8

The LORD is my portion, saith my soul; therefore will I hope in him.

LAMENTATIONS 3:24

At times my heart feels as if it has no energy left to hope with, Lord. Fear creeps in with my weariness; I hate feeling like this. I will focus on the things I know are true: Your love, Your salvation, Your care. You *will* bring good out of this.

....

....

....

....

....

....

....

....

....

Blessed be the God and Father of our Lord Jesus Christ, which according to his abundant mercy hath begotten us again unto a lively hope by the resurrection of Jesus Christ from the dead, to an inheritance incorruptible, and undefiled, and that fadeth not away, reserved in heaven for you.

1 PETER 1:3–4

For which cause we faint not; but though our outward man perish, yet the inward man is renewed day by day. For our light affliction, which is but for a moment, worketh for us a far more exceeding and eternal weight of glory; while we look not at the things which are seen, but at the things which are not seen: for the things which are seen are temporal; but the things which are not seen are eternal.

2 CORINTHIANS 4:16–18

Father, I take comfort in Your good plan for me. Just as Your Word records Your love for Your people through the ages, I can be confident that You will take care of me. My hope is safe in You; You can strengthen my heart so it overflows with joy even through my tears.

....

....

....

....

....

....

....

....

....

....

For I know the thoughts that I think toward you, saith the LORD, thoughts of peace, and not of evil, to give you an expected end.
JEREMIAH 29:11

For we know that the whole creation groaneth and travaileth in pain together until now. And not only they, but ourselves also, which have the firstfruits of the Spirit, even we ourselves groan within ourselves, waiting for the adoption, to wit, the redemption of our body. For we are saved by hope: but hope that is seen is not hope: for what a man seeth, why doth he yet hope for? But if we hope for that we see not, then do we with patience wait for it.
ROMANS 8:22–25

Joy

◆

"Count it all joy," people say encouragingly, not knowing the true extent of what you're going through. Joy doesn't mean having a smile all the time—sometimes joy looks more like gritted teeth and silent, tearful prayer. Joy isn't happiness, but instead it's a deep confidence and an abiding sense of delight in our God. No matter our circumstances, joy bubbles to the surface when our hearts are centered in His beauty, strength, and love for us. These Bible promises are full of assurance that during the tough times, God gives us reason after reason to continue persevering in joy.

The joy of the LORD is your strength.
Nehemiah 8:10

Father God, thank You that even when it feels like there is no other reason in my life to rejoice that I can take joy in You. When my heart is tired and hurting, lift my eyes to You. Show me again how Your character gives me reason to shout for joy.

....

....

....

....

....

....

....

....

....

....

....

....

But let all those that put their trust in thee rejoice:
let them ever shout for joy, because thou defendest them:
let them also that love thy name be joyful in thee.

PSALM 5:11

There be many that say, Who will shew us any good? LORD, lift thou
up the light of thy countenance upon us. Thou hast put gladness in my
heart, more than in the time that their corn and their wine increased.

PSALM 4:6–7

$\mathcal{I}$ walk in the midst of trials, trusting Your Word's promises
that You grow my faith and my patience through them;
You will preserve me and light the way for my path. If to
know Your joy more fully I must undergo this, then stay
close to me, strengthening my walking feet.

....
....
....
....
....
....
....
....
....
....
....
....
....
....

*My brethren, count it all joy when ye fall into divers temptations;
knowing this, that the trying of your faith worketh patience.*
JAMES 1:2–3

*Ye that love the LORD, hate evil: he preserveth the souls of his saints;
he delivereth them out of the hand of the wicked. Light is sown
for the righteous, and gladness for the upright in heart.*
PSALM 97:10–11

Letting Go of the Past

✦

It's hard to let go of shame and fear in our past, especially when we're haunted by terrible mistakes or have experienced horrible injustice. However long it takes, we need to let God's grace wash over these memories—there is nothing He cannot heal. If you struggle with regret, remember that Jesus has covered all your sins. For the deeply hurt, the Holy Spirit can move into the pained places of your heart and restore you by His comfort and grace. These Bible promises will encourage you to embrace the abundant life that Jesus gives when we trust in Him.

*Therefore if any man be in Christ, he is a
new creature: old things are passed away;
behold, all things are become new.*

2 Corinthians 5:17

Father, my old mistakes keep coming back to haunt me:
the things I said and did, or didn't say or left undone,
and their consequences. But You have removed these sins;
You have forgiven me. When Satan accuses me, help me say
Your truths to my heart: "I am forgiven. I am made new."

....
....
....
....
....
....
....
....
....
....
....
....
....

*For I will be merciful to their unrighteousness, and their
sins and their iniquities will I remember no more.*

HEBREWS 8:12

*For as the heaven is high above the earth, so great is his mercy
toward them that fear him. As far as the east is from the west,
so far hath he removed our transgressions from us.*

PSALM 103:11–12

Lord, on the days that shame about my past is hard to deal with, I am so thankful that Your Word tells me that I am alive in Christ! Let me see myself with new eyes, eyes that are open to see the new, beautiful work You are doing in me.

....

....

....

....

....

....

....

....

....

....

....

....

....

I am crucified with Christ: nevertheless I live; yet not I, but Christ liveth in me: and the life which I now live in the flesh I live by the faith of the Son of God, who loved me, and gave himself for me.

GALATIANS 2:20

Remember ye not the former things, neither consider the things of old. Behold, I will do a new thing; now it shall spring forth; shall ye not know it? I will even make a way in the wilderness, and rivers in the desert.

ISAIAH 43:18–19

Jesus, You have set my past behind me, hallelujah! Help me leave it there. I want to keep my eyes forward, set on You as I follow hard after You, the true prize of my life—knowing and reflecting You more and more in everything I do.

....

....

....

....

....

....

....

....

....

Wherefore seeing we also are compassed about with so great a cloud of witnesses, let us lay aside every weight, and the sin which doth so easily beset us, and let us run with patience the race that is set before us, looking unto Jesus the author and finisher of our faith; who for the joy that was set before him endured the cross, despising the shame, and is set down at the right hand of the throne of God.

HEBREWS 12:1–2

Brethren, I count not myself to have apprehended: but this one thing I do, forgetting those things which are behind, and reaching forth unto those things which are before, I press toward the mark for the prize of the high calling of God in Christ Jesus.

PHILIPPIANS 3:13–14

Loneliness

---

*O*n our healing journeys, we can feel extremely isolated, especially when people close to us don't know how to empathize with us. "How could they understand what I'm going through? They have such healthy, happy lives. I feel so alone in this." Jesus understands loneliness. He took on the ultimate isolation—separation from His beloved Father—to save us from our sins. Take courage from His name Emmanuel, which means "God with us." Ask Him for the comfort you need, whether it's understanding friends or a renewed sense of His presence. These Bible promises show that Emmanuel will never forsake you.

Whither shall I go from thy spirit? or whither shall I flee
from thy presence? If I ascend up into heaven, thou art
there: if I make my bed in hell, behold, thou art there.
If I take the wings of the morning, and dwell in the
uttermost parts of the sea; even there shall thy hand
lead me, and thy right hand shall hold me.

PSALM 139:7–10

Emmanuel, You know my loneliness. . .and You know how others have failed me in the past and why I'm hesitant to reach out. Thank You for Your nearness, for always being here. You know I long for friends, though—please lead me to good friends who are faithful and loving like You.

....

....

....

....

....

....

....

....

....

....

....

....

For the LORD will not cast off his people,
neither will he forsake his inheritance.
PSALM 94:14

They that trust in the LORD shall be as mount Zion,
which cannot be removed, but abideth for ever. As the
mountains are round about Jerusalem, so the LORD is
round about his people from henceforth even for ever.
PSALM 125:1–2

Emmanuel, I marvel at Your Word's promise that Your presence fills heaven and earth; You are never absent. When I feel lonely, help me remember that You will abide with me, no matter what— I will lift my heart up to You, trusting the love You have for me.

....

....

....

....

....

....

....

....

....

....

....

Am I a God at hand, saith the Lord, and not a God afar off?
Can any hide himself in secret places that I shall not see him?
saith the Lord. Do not I fill heaven and earth? saith the Lord.

Jeremiah 23:23–24

Whosoever shall confess that Jesus is the Son of God,
God dwelleth in him, and he in God. And we have known
and believed the love that God hath to us. God is love; and
he that dwelleth in love dwelleth in God, and God in him.

1 John 4:15–16

Loving Others

When we're in pain, it can be hard to continue showing love, whether it's to the people around us, to God, or even to ourselves. Our hearts can get so tangled up in our worries, pain, and intense emotions that it's hard to believe our love is worth anything. Remember the Father's immeasurable love for you—He fills you with His abiding love when you feel you don't have any left. Dwell on these Bible promises, knowing that the love you give—even if it doesn't feel like much—pleases the Father and blesses those with whom you share it.

Beloved, if God so loved us, we ought also to love one another. No man hath seen God at any time. If we love one another, God dwelleth in us, and his love is perfected in us.

1 JOHN 4:11–12

Loving others is daunting, Father—I don't feel like I have enough energy to get up some mornings, let alone love as You do. But thank You that godly love can grow stronger— it increases when I dwell on Your amazing affection for me. Who would You have me love today?

....
....
....
....
....
....
....
....
....
....

And we have known and believed the love that God hath to us. God is love; and he that dwelleth in love dwelleth in God, and God in him. Herein is our love made perfect, that we may have boldness in the day of judgment: because as he is, so are we in this world.

1 JOHN 4:16–17

Jesus said unto him, Thou shalt love the Lord thy God with all thy heart, and with all thy soul, and with all thy mind. This is the first and great commandment. And the second is like unto it, Thou shalt love thy neighbour as thyself. On these two commandments hang all the law and the prophets.

MATTHEW 22:37–40

Love is a higher call than simply not doing harm to others, isn't it, God? It's active and alive, nurturing and courageous. Even as I am on this healing journey, let Your love be bright and warm through me. I thank You that Your love never fails, and that You bless us when we love.

....

....

....

....

....

....

....

....

....

....

....

Charity suffereth long, and is kind; charity envieth not; charity vaunteth not itself, is not puffed up, doth not behave itself unseemly, seeketh not her own, is not easily provoked, thinketh no evil; rejoiceth not in iniquity, but rejoiceth in the truth; beareth all things, believeth all things, hopeth all things, endureth all things. Charity never faileth.

1 CORINTHIANS 13:4–8

Finally, be ye all of one mind, having compassion one of another, love as brethren, be pitiful, be courteous: not rendering evil for evil, or railing for railing: but contrariwise blessing; knowing that ye are thereunto called, that ye should inherit a blessing.

1 PETER 3:8–9

Father, withdrawing from others is tempting at times. I'm afraid I'll be rejected because of what I'm going through on this healing journey, but Your call to love transcends my fear. Cast out my fear with Your love, and help me move toward others to show them this love that makes me courageous.

....

....

....

....

....

....

....

....

....

....

....

There is no fear in love; but perfect love casteth out fear: because fear hath torment. He that feareth is not made perfect in love.

1 JOHN 4:18

Be ye therefore followers of God, as dear children; and walk in love, as Christ also hath loved us, and hath given himself for us an offering and a sacrifice to God for a sweetsmelling savour.

EPHESIANS 5:1–2

Peace

◆

The wind whips at our faces and the rain strikes us hard, yet during life's storms our hearts can be at peace if we've hidden them in Christ. We don't know what the next day or year will bring, or maybe we *do* know what hard things are coming, and we tremble at the thought. When we put our confidence in our trustworthy Savior, His peace fills and comforts us even as we see the dark clouds gathering. Read these Bible promises, and be encouraged that Jesus is the source of abiding peace; He can calm us in any storm!

Peace I leave with you, my peace I give unto you: not as the world giveth, give I unto you. Let not your heart be troubled, neither let it be afraid.

JOHN 14:27

Father, I thank You that peace is available to me, but it isn't of my making. Instead You bless me with Your peace when I tell You everything that's on my heart and let You take my burden. I open my whole heart to You today—to let Your peace come in.

....

....

....

....

....

....

....

....

....

....

....

The LORD will give strength unto his people;
the LORD will bless his people with peace.

PSALM 29:11

Be careful for nothing; but in every thing by prayer and supplication
with thanksgiving let your requests be made known unto God.
And the peace of God, which passeth all understanding, shall
keep your hearts and minds through Christ Jesus.

PHILIPPIANS 4:6–7

Lord, no matter if the earth gives way, if the doctors only
have bad news, if my healing journey takes two, ten steps
back—whatever catastrophe, whatever trouble, I trust in You.
Your faithful love gives me peace; grant me strength to
keep my heart, my confidence, set on You.

....

....

....

....

....

....

....

....

....

....

*God is our refuge and strength, a very present help in trouble.
Therefore will not we fear, though the earth be removed,
and though the mountains be carried into the midst of the sea;
though the waters thereof roar and be troubled, though the
mountains shake with the swelling thereof. Selah.*

PSALM 46:1–3

*Thou wilt keep him in perfect peace, whose mind
is stayed on thee: because he trusteth in thee.*

ISAIAH 26:3

Perseverance

---◆---

*A*fter so much work and time, we still don't see much progress in the mending of our bodies or the restoration of our broken relationships. It's so tempting to give up when it seems like nothing is improving. Don't give up—Jesus will help you continue on. Perseverance means choosing to trust Jesus and continue following Him even on the darkest, hardest days. These Bible promises will show you how God will provide what you need to persevere—His strength, and most importantly, His presence. No matter how long your journey is, remember that every step forward is a victory.

Therefore, my beloved brethren, be ye stedfast,
unmoveable, always abounding in the work
of the Lord, forasmuch as ye know that your
labour is not in vain in the Lord.

1 Corinthians 15:58

Jesus, Your Word promises that You are constantly at work in Your people; You'll keep on keeping until I'm perfected in You. I want to reflect this characteristic of Yours in my life—practicing perseverance in my healing journey. Thank You that You will never leave Your good work in me unfinished!

....

....

....

....

....

....

....

....

....

....

....

....

Being confident of this very thing, that he which hath begun a good work in you will perform it until the day of Jesus Christ.

PHILIPPIANS 1:6

The LORD will perfect that which concerneth me: thy mercy, O LORD, endureth for ever: forsake not the works of thine own hands.

PSALM 138:8

It's getting to me, Father. Whether it's PT exercises, hashing more stuff out in therapy, or summoning the courage for hard conversations, the work is never done. But You establish the work of my hands; You will bring Your good work (and mine) to completion. Strengthen me, Lord. Help me persevere.

....

....

....

....

....

....

....

....

....

....

....

And let us not be weary in well doing:
for in due season we shall reap, if we faint not.
GALATIANS 6:9

Therefore, brethren, stand fast, and hold the traditions which ye have
been taught, whether by word, or our epistle. Now our Lord Jesus
Christ himself, and God, even our Father, which hath loved us, and
hath given us everlasting consolation and good hope through grace,
comfort your hearts, and stablish you in every good word and work.
2 THESSALONIANS 2:15–17

Lord, today perseverance feels more like waiting for this to be over, to endure just a little bit longer. I honestly don't know how much more I can take. Right now, please comfort my weary heart with Your mercy and Your promise to use everything, even this, for my good and for Your glory.

....

....

....

....

....

....

....

....

....

....

....

....

*Behold, we count them happy which endure. Ye have heard
of the patience of Job, and have seen the end of the Lord;
that the Lord is very pitiful, and of tender mercy.*

JAMES 5:11

*And not only so, but we glory in tribulations also: knowing that
tribulation worketh patience; and patience, experience; and experience,
hope: and hope maketh not ashamed; because the love of God is shed
abroad in our hearts by the Holy Ghost which is given unto us.*

ROMANS 5:3–5

Prayer

◆

*P*rayer is one of the most precious gifts our heavenly Father has given us. Through Jesus, we are invited to come boldly into God's presence and tell Him everything that's going on in our lives. Prayer is a holy practice that is essential to our lives and our healing journey. Even if He doesn't change what's happening in our lives right away, through prayer and scripture God strengthens us to hold on to Him and His great love. Hold fast to these Bible promises as you come in humble faith to the Father and pour out all your needs before Him!

Let us therefore come boldly unto the throne of grace, that we may obtain mercy, and find grace to help in time of need.

HEBREWS 4:16

Father, sometimes I hesitate to pray, feeling weary or wordless. But You invite me to come to You, no matter how I feel, and when my words dry up, Your Spirit intercedes for me. Thank You for always welcoming me into Your presence, that You delight in listening when I pray.

....

....

....

....

....

....

....

....

....

....

And this is the confidence that we have in him, that, if we ask any thing according to his will, he heareth us: and if we know that he hear us, whatsoever we ask, we know that we have the petitions that we desired of him.

1 John 5:14–15

Likewise the Spirit also helpeth our infirmities: for we know not what we should pray for as we ought: but the Spirit itself maketh intercession for us with groanings which cannot be uttered. And he that searcheth the hearts knoweth what is the mind of the Spirit, because he maketh intercession for the saints according to the will of God.

Romans 8:26–27

Lord, though I cry out what feels like the same prayer day after day, I'm encouraged, for Your Word reminds me to be persistent in prayer—to keep bringing You my needs and fears, because You hear. You love. You answer. Help me grow in persistence, to daily surrender these burdens to You.

....

....

....

....

....

....

....

....

*Evening, and morning, and at noon, will I pray,
and cry aloud: and he shall hear my voice.*

PSALM 55:17

*And he spake a parable unto them to this end, that men ought always
to pray, and not to faint; saying, There was in a city a judge, which
feared not God, neither regarded man: and there was a widow in that
city; and she came unto him, saying, Avenge me of mine adversary. And
he would not for a while: but afterward he said within himself, Though
I fear not God, nor regard man; yet because this widow troubleth me,
I will avenge her, lest by her continual coming she weary me. And the
Lord said, Hear what the unjust judge saith. And shall not God avenge
his own elect, which cry day and night unto him, though he bear long
with them? I tell you that he will avenge them speedily. Nevertheless
when the Son of man cometh, shall he find faith on the earth?*

LUKE 18:1–8

Provision

One of God's names is *Jehovah-jireh*, which means "The Lord Who Provides." Throughout scripture, we read about how God provided for the tangible and intangible needs of His people—He sent manna from heaven for the Israelites' hunger, and He sent Jesus to fill the spiritual hunger of our hearts. Through Christ, we can come before the Father boldly, carrying all our petitions for healing, for financial help, for strength to endure. He calls us to wait on Him in faith, but He doesn't leave His children desolate. These Bible promises show how God listens and answers His people's prayers for provision.

And I say unto you, ask, and it shall be given you; seek, and ye shall find; knock, and it shall be opened unto you. For every one that asketh receiveth; and he that seeketh findeth; and to him that knocketh it shall be opened. If a son shall ask bread of any of you that is a father, will he give him a stone? or if he ask a fish, will he for a fish give him a serpent? Or if he shall ask an egg, will he offer him a scorpion? If ye then, being evil, know how to give good gifts unto your children: how much more shall your heavenly Father give the Holy Spirit to them that ask him?

Luke 11:9–13

Father, I struggle to believe Your promise of provision when I see the bills, my family's needs. I don't know what to pray, other than this: look on Your child and have mercy, Jehovah-jireh. I choose to believe Your Word and press into Your bountiful grace, waiting for Your provision.

....

....

....

....

....

....

....

....

....

....

Therefore take no thought, saying, What shall we eat? or, What shall we drink? or, Wherewithal shall we be clothed? (For after all these things do the Gentiles seek:) for your heavenly Father knoweth that ye have need of all these things. But seek ye first the kingdom of God, and his righteousness; and all these things shall be added unto you.

MATTHEW 6:31–33

The young lions do lack, and suffer hunger: but they that seek the LORD shall not want any good thing.

PSALM 34:10

The picture of You as a shepherd tenderly caring for Your flock is a comfort to my soul, Lord. Just as the shepherd feeds, waters, and protects the sheep, You also care for the daily details of my life. Nothing escapes Your notice; help me to trust You with my needs.

....

....

....

....

....

....

....

....

....

....

The LORD is my shepherd; I shall not want. He maketh me to lie down in green pastures: he leadeth me beside the still waters. He restoreth my soul: he leadeth me in the paths of righteousness for his name's sake.

PSALM 23:1–3

Behold, the Lord GOD will come with strong hand, and his arm shall rule for him: behold, his reward is with him, and his work before him. He shall feed his flock like a shepherd: he shall gather the lambs with his arm, and carry them in his bosom, and shall gently lead those that are with young.

ISAIAH 40:10–11

Father, when fear strikes and lack threatens, bring to my
mind the "benefits" that You have supplied in the past,
and teach my heart to trust Your promise to provide in
the future! Thank You that You are a God of abundance,
not a God who has to budget to make ends meet.

....

....

....

....

....

....

....

....

....

....

....

....

*Bless the LORD, O my soul, and forget not all
his benefits: . . .who satisfieth thy mouth with good
things; so that thy youth is renewed like the eagle's.*
PSALM 103:2, 5

*But my God shall supply all your need according
to his riches in glory by Christ Jesus.*
PHILIPPIANS 4:19

Questioning and Doubts

◆

When we walk through pain, doubt and uncertainty can quietly creep in. "Why does God have me going through this? Right now I'm having a lot of trouble believing He's on my side." Thankfully, we can bring all of our questions, hurt, and doubts to Him. God can handle anything we ask Him, and He'll answer us wisely according to our need. Think of Gideon and his fleece (Judges 6), or Thomas declaring he needed to touch Jesus' wounds to believe (John 20:25). These Bible promises show that God will reach out to us in our doubt and give us hope.

Why sayest thou, O Jacob, and speakest, O Israel, My way is hid from the Lord, and my judgment is passed over from my God? Hast thou not known? hast thou not heard, that the everlasting God, the Lord, the Creator of the ends of the earth, fainteth not, neither is weary? there is no searching of his understanding. He giveth power to the faint; and to them that have no might he increaseth strength.

Isaiah 40:27–29

Jesus, today I echo the prayer of the father of the sick child in Mark 9: I believe; help my unbelief. Your kindness to doubters in scripture encourages me; thank You for not turning them—or me—away. Increase my faith, dear Savior, even as I bring my questions and doubts to You.

....

....

....

....

....

Jesus said unto him, If thou canst believe, all things are possible to him that believeth. And straightway the father of the child cried out, and said with tears, Lord, I believe; help thou mine unbelief.

MARK 9:23–24

But Thomas, one of the twelve, called Didymus, was not with them when Jesus came. The other disciples therefore said unto him, We have seen the LORD. But he said unto them, Except I shall see in his hands the print of the nails, and put my finger into the print of the nails, and thrust my hand into his side, I will not believe. And after eight days again his disciples were within, and Thomas with them: then came Jesus, the doors being shut, and stood in the midst, and said, Peace be unto you. Then saith he to Thomas, Reach hither thy finger, and behold my hands; and reach hither thy hand, and thrust it into my side: and be not faithless, but believing. And Thomas answered and said unto him, My LORD and my God. Jesus saith unto him, Thomas, because thou hast seen me, thou hast believed: blessed are they that have not seen, and yet have believed.

JOHN 20:24–29

Father God, though my doubts sometimes spin in my heart like debris in a hurricane, Your character is firm; You never abandon Your people. Thank You for Your constancy and love! I bring You my questions and doubts, knowing that You will accept me as I am because of Jesus.

....

....

....

....

....

....

....

....

....

....

It is a faithful saying: For if we be dead with him, we shall also live with him: if we suffer, we shall also reign with him: if we deny him, he also will deny us: if we believe not, yet he abideth faithful: he cannot deny himself.

2 Timothy 2:11–13

But Zion said, The Lord hath forsaken me, and my Lord hath forgotten me. Can a woman forget her sucking child, that she should not have compassion on the son of her womb? yea, they may forget, yet will I not forget thee.

Isaiah 49:14–15

Questioning My Purpose

*Y*our whole world changes when you're going through extreme illness or trauma—old routines are traded in for doctor visits, treatments, and waiting for normalcy to return. If your condition persists, it's easy to question what your purpose is—"How can I do any good when I'm like this?" Though life has changed drastically, you are still an important part of God's family. These Bible promises show that God has planned out good work for you to do in His kingdom. Though you may feel limited, He'll give you wisdom to understand how to serve Him faithfully during this time.

Ye are the light of the world. A city that is set on an hill cannot be hid. Neither do men light a candle, and put it under a bushel, but on a candlestick; and it giveth light unto all that are in the house. Let your light so shine before men, that they may see your good works, and glorify your Father which is in heaven.

Matthew 5:14–16

This need for healing has turned my life upside down, Lord. I can't see the path ahead, or even who I'm supposed to be. But You have a good plan for me—I choose to trust Your love. Though all else has changed, remind me that my true, deep-down identity is only found in Christ.

....

....

....

....

....

....

....

....

....

....

For we are his workmanship, created in Christ Jesus unto good works, which God hath before ordained that we should walk in them.

EPHESIANS 2:10

For I know the thoughts that I think toward you, saith the LORD, thoughts of peace, and not of evil, to give you an expected end. Then shall ye call upon me, and ye shall go and pray unto me, and I will hearken unto you. And ye shall seek me, and find me, when ye shall search for me with all your heart.

JEREMIAH 29:11–13

Father, I'm wrestling with the lie that because I cannot work as hard or in the ways I used to, I've lost my purpose. Please comfort my heart; remind me that You love me regardless of how "productive" I am, and abiding in You is what enables me to bear lasting fruit.

....

....

....

....

....

....

....

....

....

I am the vine, ye are the branches: He that abideth in me, and I in him, the same bringeth forth much fruit: for without me ye can do nothing. . . . If ye abide in me, and my words abide in you, ye shall ask what ye will, and it shall be done unto you. Herein is my Father glorified, that ye bear much fruit; so shall ye be my disciples.

JOHN 15:5, 7–8

Looking for that blessed hope, and the glorious appearing of the great God and our Saviour Jesus Christ; who gave himself for us, that he might redeem us from all iniquity, and purify unto himself a peculiar people, zealous of good works.

TITUS 2:13–14

Father, my resources, time, and energy feel so limited. I know my healing journey doesn't stop me from being a member of Your kingdom, but I don't know what my role looks like now. By Your grace, encourage me that You have ways for me to glorify You even now.

....

....

....

....

....

....

....

....

....

....

And God is able to make all grace abound toward you; that ye, always having all sufficiency in all things, may abound to every good work.
2 CORINTHIANS 9:8

I have planted, Apollos watered; but God gave the increase. So then neither is he that planteth any thing, neither he that watereth; but God that giveth the increase. Now he that planteth and he that watereth are one: and every man shall receive his own reward according to his own labour. For we are labourers together with God: ye are God's husbandry, ye are God's building.
1 CORINTHIANS 3:6–9

Reconciliation

*R*econciliation is seeking to restore a relationship that's been broken. Just as we follow Jesus' example for when we forgive others, we look to Him for reconciliation too—He brought us back to God through His sacrifice, and the Holy Spirit helps us to reconcile to one another. Sometimes it takes years for a relationship to heal. Sometimes reconciliation means that the relationship must end, but it ends in peace. Read these Bible promises, and be encouraged by your Savior's example, remembering that we depend on the power of the Spirit to heal relationships and change people's hearts.

For if, when we were enemies, we were reconciled to God by the death of his Son, much more, being reconciled, we shall be saved by his life.

ROMANS 5:10

Father, I've told You of the pain I carry in my heart because of someone who hurt me deeply. I've been holding back from confronting that person because I know how hard the conversation will be. Please provide the courage and love I need to approach them so our relationship can be restored.

....

....

....

....

....

....

....

....

....

....

Moreover if thy brother shall trespass against thee, go and tell him his fault between thee and him alone: if he shall hear thee, thou hast gained thy brother. But if he will not hear thee, then take with thee one or two more, that in the mouth of two or three witnesses every word may be established. And if he shall neglect to hear them, tell it unto the church: but if he neglect to hear the church, let him be unto thee as an heathen man and a publican.

MATTHEW 18:15–17

Forbearing one another, and forgiving one another, if any man have a quarrel against any: even as Christ forgave you, so also do ye.

COLOSSIANS 3:13

Jesus, it's only because of Your sacrifice that true reconciliation is possible! And then You extended the ministry of reconciliation to Your children, to me. Help me be a peacemaker—whether that means asking forgiveness or offering it—with an open, willing heart, trusting You to ultimately heal my relationships.

....

....

....

....

....

....

....

....

....

....

*And, having made peace through the blood of his cross,
by him to reconcile all things unto himself; by him, I say,
whether they be things in earth, or things in heaven.*

COLOSSIANS 1:20

*And all things are of God, who hath reconciled us to himself
by Jesus Christ, and hath given to us the ministry of reconciliation;
to wit, that God was in Christ, reconciling the world unto
himself, not imputing their trespasses unto them; and hath
committed unto us the word of reconciliation.*

2 CORINTHIANS 5:18–19

Lord, I've tried to make amends, but this relationship has changed, maybe forever. I've done all I can, but it hurts so much. Help me to leave it in Your hands and pray for the other person involved—You know both our hearts, and please grant us clarity and peace.

....

....

....

....

....

....

....

....

....

....

....

Bless them that curse you, and pray for them which despitefully use you.

LUKE 6:28

Therefore judge nothing before the time, until the Lord come, who both will bring to light the hidden things of darkness, and will make manifest the counsels of the hearts: and then shall every man have praise of God.

1 CORINTHIANS 4:5

Repentance

◆

When we sin, repentance is necessary to heal the break in our relationship with God and those we've sinned against. When we repent, we choose to turn away from that sin, and our heart's desire is to never repeat it again, doing our best not to as we struggle with our sin nature on this side of heaven. As God's redeemed children, we please our holy Father when we repent and seek to follow His ways in our lives. In these Bible promises, you will see that when we repent, God is faithful and just to forgive us.

Draw nigh to God, and he will draw nigh to you.
Cleanse your hands, ye sinners; and purify your
hearts, ye double minded. Be afflicted, and mourn,
and weep: let your laughter be turned to mourning,
and your joy to heaviness. Humble yourselves in
the sight of the Lord, and he shall lift you up.

JAMES 4:8–10

God, You know the sins that I wrestle with. You want my whole heart to be set on You and what You love—help me to have a broken heart over my sin and turn away from it, for that pleases You. Thank You for Your mercy, kindness, and forgiveness.

....

....

....

....

....

....

....

....

....

....

....

For thou desirest not sacrifice; else would I give it: thou delightest not in burnt offering. The sacrifices of God are a broken spirit: a broken and a contrite heart, O God, thou wilt not despise.

PSALM 51:16–17

Therefore also now, saith the LORD, turn ye even to me with all your heart, and with fasting, and with weeping, and with mourning: and rend your heart, and not your garments, and turn unto the LORD your God: for he is gracious and merciful, slow to anger, and of great kindness, and repenteth him of the evil.

JOEL 2:12–13

Father, even as I come to You feeling sorrowful about my sin, I am gladdened by the truth that You rejoice over my repentance. When I feel weighed down by conviction, remind me that the joy from repenting will lighten my load. My righteousness doesn't cut it—Yours is what I need.

....

....

....

....

....

....

....

....

....

....

....

For godly sorrow worketh repentance to salvation not to be repented of: but the sorrow of the world worketh death.

2 Corinthians 7:10

I say unto you, that likewise joy shall be in heaven over one sinner that repenteth, more than over ninety and nine just persons, which need no repentance.

Luke 15:7

Father, I often want to push my sins aside, to pretend they aren't there, but that leads to restless thoughts and creeping guilt. Your mercy is rich and never withheld. . . Why do I forget it so easily? Wash me and strengthen me to walk in Your ways on my healing journey.

He that covereth his sins shall not prosper: but whoso confesseth and forsaketh them shall have mercy.

PROVERBS 28:13

Seek ye the LORD while he may be found, call ye upon him while he is near: let the wicked forsake his way, and the unrighteous man his thoughts: and let him return unto the LORD, and he will have mercy upon him; and to our God, for he will abundantly pardon.

ISAIAH 55:6–7

Rest

———◆———

We crave physical and spiritual rest. It's such a comfort that we can rest in Jesus! To rest in Him means we set our worries aside to stand firm on His unchanging promises. Through His free gift of salvation, we have the unshakeable hope of eternity with Him. Here on earth, we know that He hears and answers us when we pray. When we surrender everything to Him—fears, dreams, and hopes—His rest permeates our hearts and gives solace to our bodies. Let these Bible promises fill you with confidence that Jesus provides heart-deep rest for His people.

*Come unto me, all ye that labour and are heavy laden,
and I will give you rest. Take my yoke upon you,
and learn of me; for I am meek and lowly in heart:
and ye shall find rest unto your souls.*

MATTHEW 11:28–29

When the enemy accuses me, saying I'm unworthy to be Your child, that You do not really love me, Your Spirit whispers, "No. I know all things, and You belong to Jesus because of what He has done. That will never change." Jesus, help my soul rest in the promise of Your salvation.

....

....

....

....

....

....

....

....

....

....

There remaineth therefore a rest to the people of God. For he that is entered into his rest, he also hath ceased from his own works, as God did from his. Let us labour therefore to enter into that rest, lest any man fall after the same example of unbelief.

HEBREWS 4:9–11

My little children, let us not love in word, neither in tongue; but in deed and in truth. And hereby we know that we are of the truth, and shall assure our hearts before him. For if our heart condemn us, God is greater than our heart, and knoweth all things.

I JOHN 3:18–20

Lord, to rest in Your presence in the midst of my day's demands, to draw in Your peace and love as a branch does nutrients from the vine—this is my desire. I can rest because I know You hold my life, the entire universe, in place. Whatever may happen, You are faithful.

....

....

....

....

....

....

....

....

....

....

....

....

Abide in me, and I in you. As the branch cannot bear fruit of itself, except it abide in the vine; no more can ye, except ye abide in me. I am the vine, ye are the branches: He that abideth in me, and I in him, the same bringeth forth much fruit: for without me ye can do nothing.

JOHN 15:4–5

The fear of the LORD tendeth to life: and he that hath it shall abide satisfied; he shall not be visited with evil.

PROVERBS 19:23

You have seen my restless nights, El Roi, the God who sees. Some nights it's the medication, the pain; others it's the worries, the nightmares. I know You are near whether I'm awake or sleeping, faithfully caring for me. Bless me with rest, dear Provider, and if not that, the strength to keep going.

....

....

....

....

....

....

....

....

....

....

....

....

I will both lay me down in peace, and sleep:
for thou, LORD, only makest me dwell in safety.

PSALM 4:8

They that trust in the LORD shall be as mount Zion, which
cannot be removed, but abideth for ever. As the mountains
are round about Jerusalem, so the LORD is round about
his people from henceforth even for ever.

PSALM 125:1–2

Rewriting Your Story

———◆———

O ur lives are intertwined in God's vast theme of redemption that we see woven in His Word. We can't simply brush our suffering aside, but we can search out His redemption in our healing journeys. We can choose to tell our stories through the vision of joy, with our eyes open to witness and retell God's mercy and goodness to us. We can reframe our painful tale in hope, trusting that God will show us the beauty He's bringing out of our circumstances. Meditate on these Bible promises about God's redemption, and take courage to begin rewriting your story.

They that sow in tears shall reap in joy. He that goeth forth and weepeth, bearing precious seed, shall doubtless come again with rejoicing, bringing his sheaves with him.

PSALM 126:5–6

It's easy to look at my life through the lens of pain, but I want to look for the good You promise. It will be hard, but I trust You— You can transform my thinking and write wholeness into my story. You can make anything beautiful—it's the kind of God You are.

....

....

....

....

....

....

....

....

....

....

....

And he hath put a new song in my mouth, even praise unto our God: many shall see it, and fear, and shall trust in the LORD.

PSALM 40:3

Bless the LORD, O my soul: and all that is within me, bless his holy name. Bless the LORD, O my soul, and forget not all his benefits: who forgiveth all thine iniquities; who healeth all thy diseases; who redeemeth thy life from destruction; who crowneth thee with lovingkindness and tender mercies; who satisfieth thy mouth with good things; so that thy youth is renewed like the eagle's.

PSALM 103:1–5

Father, these Bible promises about heaven and newness fill me with such hope. You are already working to restore, to rebuild, and it will be completed when I see You face to face. As You redeem my past, my present, my future, give me eyes to see it and Your faithfulness in it all.

....

....

....

....

....

....

....

....

....

....

....

*And he that sat upon the throne said, Behold, I make all things new.
And he said unto me, Write: for these words are true and faithful.*

REVELATION 21:5

*Remember ye not the former things, neither consider the
things of old. Behold, I will do a new thing; now it shall
spring forth; shall ye not know it? I will even make
a way in the wilderness, and rivers in the desert.*

ISAIAH 43:18–19

Lord, Joseph spoke the truth: You work good in our lives even from the evil others perpetrate. Just as Christ was brought to the cross by people who hated Him, His death led to the hope of our salvation. Help me to recognize it—and praise— when You're rewriting my story for my good.

....

....

....

....

....

....

....

....

....

....

And Joseph said unto them, Fear not: for am I in the place of God? But as for you, ye thought evil against me; but God meant it unto good, to bring to pass, as it is this day, to save much people alive. Now therefore fear ye not: I will nourish you, and your little ones. And he comforted them, and spake kindly unto them.

GENESIS 50:19–21

Therefore we are buried with him by baptism into death: that like as Christ was raised up from the dead by the glory of the Father, even so we also should walk in newness of life.

ROMANS 6:4

Salvation

Our salvation through Christ is the bedrock of our lives and our hope for the future. He conquered sin and death by the power of His resurrection, and that same life-giving power moves in our lives. We don't have to fear what may happen in life, because He's promised to walk it with us. We don't have to fear death, because our salvation is secure, and Jesus will help us make that crossing when it's time. When you need assurance, remember these Bible promises—no matter what happens, nothing can snatch you out of the Father's hand.

For God so loved the world, that he gave his only begotten Son, that whosoever believeth in him should not perish, but have everlasting life. For God sent not his Son into the world to condemn the world; but that the world through him might be saved.

JOHN 3:16–17

Dear Jesus, thank You for filling the thirst in my soul
with Living Water, Your salvation. You are the Good
Shepherd who laid down Your life for the sheep—and
You leave none of us behind. Remind me when I thirst,
when I feel lost, that You are faithful evermore.

....

....

....

....

....

....

....

....

....

....

*Jesus answered and said unto her, Whosoever drinketh of this water
shall thirst again: but whosoever drinketh of the water that I shall
give him shall never thirst; but the water that I shall give him shall
be in him a well of water springing up into everlasting life.*

JOHN 4:13–14

*My sheep hear my voice, and I know them, and they follow me:
and I give unto them eternal life; and they shall never perish,
neither shall any man pluck them out of my hand. My Father,
which gave them me, is greater than all; and no man is able
to pluck them out of my Father's hand.*

JOHN 10:27–29

Father, I've watched earthly things fall apart—You know what's pulling apart at the seams in my life, what has grieved and distressed me. Through my hurt, keep me centered on my "lively hope," my place in Your "holy nation" that has received mercy. Your promise of salvation will never fail. Amen!

....

....

....

....

....

....

....

....

Blessed be the God and Father of our Lord Jesus Christ, which according to his abundant mercy hath begotten us again unto a lively hope by the resurrection of Jesus Christ from the dead, to an inheritance incorruptible, and undefiled, and that fadeth not away, reserved in heaven for you, who are kept by the power of God through faith unto salvation ready to be revealed in the last time.

1 PETER 1:3–5

But ye are a chosen generation, a royal priesthood, an holy nation, a peculiar people; that ye should shew forth the praises of him who hath called you out of darkness into his marvellous light; which in time past were not a people, but are now the people of God: which had not obtained mercy, but now have obtained mercy.

1 PETER 2:9–10

Jesus, I long for heaven, to be with You and wholly healed. But until You call me, let me be focused on You, the One who never leaves me, who holds my soul in safety. Help me live as one whose hope is secure—one who is victorious in Your salvation.

....

....

....

....

....

....

....

....

....

....

....

Jesus said unto her, I am the resurrection, and the life: he that believeth in me, though he were dead, yet shall he live: and whosoever liveth and believeth in me shall never die. Believest thou this?

JOHN 11:25–26

So when this corruptible shall have put on incorruption, and this mortal shall have put on immortality, then shall be brought to pass the saying that is written, Death is swallowed up in victory. O death, where is thy sting? O grave, where is thy victory? The sting of death is sin; and the strength of sin is the law. But thanks be to God, which giveth us the victory through our Lord Jesus Christ.

1 CORINTHIANS 15:54–57

Shame

◆

Shame is that small, sinister voice in your heart that whispers to you that you're deeply flawed and undeserving of love. "If they knew what you're *really* like. . .if they knew what you've done. . ." Shame makes you want to hide, but you don't have to. When Jesus saved you, He took on your shame as well as your sin. Neither your past nor present failings can undo the fact that Jesus has made you a new creation! Absorb these Bible promises, so when you hear shame's whispering voice, you can answer with the truth: "In Christ, I am loved and redeemed."

There is therefore now no condemnation to them which are in Christ Jesus, who walk not after the flesh, but after the Spirit. For the law of the Spirit of life in Christ Jesus hath made me free from the law of sin and death.

ROMANS 8:1–2

Lord, sometimes shame reminds me of things I've done wrong, and it makes me want to hide. I have no reason to, though, because of Jesus' forgiveness; He loves me more than I could ever know. When shame speaks up, help me trust Jesus' saving work, and that He'll help me grow to be like Him.

....

....

....

....

....

....

....

....

....

....

*Even as Christ also loved the church, and gave himself for it;
that he might sanctify and cleanse it with the washing of
water by the word, that he might present it to himself a
glorious church, not having spot, or wrinkle, or any such
thing; but that it should be holy and without blemish.*

EPHESIANS 5:25–27

*Come now, and let us reason together, saith the LORD:
though your sins be as scarlet, they shall be as white as snow;
though they be red like crimson, they shall be as wool.*

ISAIAH 1:18

It's easy to dwell on the parts of myself I wish weren't there. But You love me entirely—with perfect love. I need help to see myself the way You do: fully accepted because of Christ. Please help me corral these thoughts when they attack, and send them off in light of Your truth.

....
....
....
....
....
....
....
....
....
....

(For the weapons of our warfare are not carnal, but mighty through God to the pulling down of strong holds;) casting down imaginations, and every high thing that exalteth itself against the knowledge of God, and bringing into captivity every thought to the obedience of Christ.

2 CORINTHIANS 10:4–5

Finally, brethren, whatsoever things are true, whatsoever things are honest, whatsoever things are just, whatsoever things are pure, whatsoever things are lovely, whatsoever things are of good report; if there be any virtue, and if there be any praise, think on these things.

PHILIPPIANS 4:8

My battle with shame is ongoing, Father, but I am not defeated, for You are with me. As I gaze at You, You show me the truth about myself, who You created me to be, truth that holds shame at bay. I rejoice in the freedom and salvation You bring!

....

....

....

....

....

....

....

....

....

....

....

I will greatly rejoice in the LORD, my soul shall be joyful in my God;
for he hath clothed me with the garments of salvation, he hath covered
me with the robe of righteousness, as a bridegroom decketh himself
with ornaments, and as a bride adorneth herself with her jewels.

ISAIAH 61:10

Now the Lord is that Spirit: and where the Spirit of the Lord is,
there is liberty. But we all, with open face beholding as in a
glass the glory of the Lord, are changed into the same image
from glory to glory, even as by the Spirit of the Lord.

2 CORINTHIANS 3:17–18

Strength

◆

*S*tress saps our strength when we face a multitude of troubles—medical bills, heavy family obligations, persistent pain, sleepless nights. God doesn't expect us to accomplish everything on our own. He also doesn't ask us to "do the best we can" and only after we're exhausted will He step in to assist. God promises His nearness in every moment of our lives and gives us grace to trust that He will generously provide strength to us in our time of need. In these Bible promises, we see how God continually strengthens those who have put their confidence in Him.

Hast thou not known? hast thou not heard, that the everlasting God, the LORD, the Creator of the ends of the earth, fainteth not, neither is weary? there is no searching of his understanding. He giveth power to the faint; and to them that have no might he increaseth strength. Even the youths shall faint and be weary, and the young men shall utterly fall: but they that wait upon the LORD shall renew their strength; they shall mount up with wings as eagles; they shall run, and not be weary; and they shall walk, and not faint.

Isaiah 40:28–31

Today I need an extra measure of strength, Lord. There's a lot that needs to be done and hardly any time to do it. Thank You that I can lean on Your strength—You enable me to do everything You've called me to. Just. . .help me to see what is necessary.

....

....

....

....

....

....

....

....

....

....

....

....

....

....

....

O love the LORD, all ye his saints: for the LORD preserveth the faithful, and plentifully rewardeth the proud doer. Be of good courage, and he shall strengthen your heart, all ye that hope in the LORD.

PSALM 31:23–24

The LORD God is my strength, and he will make my feet like hinds' feet, and he will make me to walk upon mine high places.

HABAKKUK 3:19

Lord, You see me struggling, the days compounding into months. This long journey toward healing is taking it out of me; my own power and my emotional energy feel all spent. Give me Your strength and guidance to keep going. Thank You that You will never leave me on my own.

....

....

....

....

....

....

....

....

....

....

....

....

The Lord is my light and my salvation; whom shall I fear?
the Lord is the strength of my life; of whom shall I be afraid?
PSALM 27:1

For who is God save the Lord? or who is a rock save our God?
It is God that girdeth me with strength, and maketh my way perfect.
PSALM 18:31–32

Trouble surrounds—my daily needs mounting, tears
springing to my eyes, but You are faithful and true, Father.
You promise to provide the power I need to endure,
to be content, and to follow You. All I feel is my
weakness. . . . please hold me up with Your strong hand.

....
....
....
....
....
....
....
....
....
....
....
....

*Fear thou not; for I am with thee: be not dismayed; for I am
thy God: I will strengthen thee; yea, I will help thee; yea,
I will uphold thee with the right hand of my righteousness.*
Isaiah 41:10

I can do all things through Christ which strengtheneth me.
Philippians 4:13

Suffering

---

*H*ow do we cope with suffering? The Bible is filled with promises for those who suffer—our suffering is not meaningless, and we can learn to follow Christ better through our painful experiences. Jesus endured physical pain, emotional distress, and spiritual devastation when He was separated from His Father on the cross, yet He remained obedient. Our Savior understands what we feel and will comfort us, giving us the strength to persevere. May these Bible promises fill you with hope—for consolation through the Spirit, and strength to endure until God's glorious purpose for us is revealed.

For which cause we faint not; but though our outward man perish, yet the inward man is renewed day by day. For our light affliction, which is but for a moment, worketh for us a far more exceeding and eternal weight of glory; while we look not at the things which are seen, but at the things which are not seen: for the things which are seen are temporal; but the things which are not seen are eternal.

2 CORINTHIANS 4:16–18

Jesus, it is hard to praise through this suffering; I want to be obedient. . .show me how. Thank You for the promise that Your power is displayed through my weakness. Help me hold on to You and the sure hope that You use everything to make me more like You.

....

....

....

....

....

....

....

And lest I should be exalted above measure through the abundance of the revelations, there was given to me a thorn in the flesh, the messenger of Satan to buffet me, lest I should be exalted above measure. For this thing I besought the Lord thrice, that it might depart from me. And he said unto me, My grace is sufficient for thee: for my strength is made perfect in weakness. Most gladly therefore will I rather glory in my infirmities, that the power of Christ may rest upon me. Therefore I take pleasure in infirmities, in reproaches, in necessities, in persecutions, in distresses for Christ's sake: for when I am weak, then am I strong.

2 CORINTHIANS 12:7–10

And not only so, but we glory in tribulations also: knowing that tribulation worketh patience; and patience, experience; and experience, hope: and hope maketh not ashamed; because the love of God is shed abroad in our hearts by the Holy Ghost which is given unto us.

ROMANS 5:3–5

161

Tender Father, I feel like I've reached my limit, hit the wall of how much I can take. I don't have anything left. All I have is You. Lift these tired eyes to see You; open these cracked lips to praise You, my hope, my sustainer. I entrust my suffering heart to You.

....

....

....

....

....

....

....

....

....

....

....

....

Wherefore let them that suffer according to the will of God commit the keeping of their souls to him in well doing, as unto a faithful Creator.

1 Peter 4:19

For I know that my redeemer liveth, and that he shall stand at the latter day upon the earth: and though after my skin worms destroy this body, yet in my flesh shall I see God: whom I shall see for myself, and mine eyes shall behold, and not another; though my reins be consumed within me.

Job 19:25–27

Jesus, one of the things that jumps out in Your Word is how You—sinless, selfless—suffered for us to bring us salvation. It hurts so much, this suffering, but if You will use it to reveal Your beauty in me, then lead me on, dear Savior. I know that You are faithful.

....

....

....

....

....

....

....

....

....

....

....

....

....

But if, when ye do well, and suffer for it, ye take it patiently, this is acceptable with God. For even hereunto were ye called: because Christ also suffered for us, leaving us an example, that ye should follow his steps: who did no sin, neither was guile found in his mouth.

1 PETER 2:20–22

For I reckon that the sufferings of this present time are not worthy to be compared with the glory which shall be revealed in us.

ROMANS 8:18

Temptation

◆

*I*n the moment we are tempted, we must choose— will we decide to obey God or to turn away from what pleases Him? On our healing journeys, temptation can come from all sides—we might be tempted to be angry with God or to despair, or to react to our pain by hurting those around us. Just as God is gracious to forgive us, He also gives us grace for our times of temptation. Read these Bible promises that show how God provided a way to combat temptation and Satan's lies by giving us His True Word to guide us.

Blessed is the man that endureth temptation: for when he is tried, he shall receive the crown of life, which the Lord hath promised to them that love him.

JAMES 1:12

Lord, thank You for Your promise that there is always an escape from temptation. Strengthen my discernment, the eyes of my heart, to look for that escape hatch and to want to take it. Train me to love You and Your Word more than the sin that would entrap me.

....

....

....

....

....

....

....

....

....

....

....

....

There hath no temptation taken you but such as is common to man: but God is faithful, who will not suffer you to be tempted above that ye are able; but will with the temptation also make a way to escape, that ye may be able to bear it.

1 CORINTHIANS 10:13

The fear of the LORD is a fountain of life, to depart from the snares of death.

PROVERBS 14:27

Jesus, I take comfort that You have "been there": You know what it's like to be tempted, and so You are gentle with me when I struggle with sin. Help me listen to Your Spirit when temptation comes—thank You that You promise grace and mercy in my time of need!

....

....

....

....

....

....

....

....

....

....

Seeing then that we have a great high priest, that is passed into the heavens, Jesus the Son of God, let us hold fast our profession. For we have not an high priest which cannot be touched with the feeling of our infirmities; but was in all points tempted like as we are, yet without sin. Let us therefore come boldly unto the throne of grace, that we may obtain mercy, and find grace to help in time of need.

HEBREWS 4:14–16

The Lord knoweth how to deliver the godly out of temptations, and to reserve the unjust unto the day of judgment to be punished.

2 PETER 2:9

Lord, I feel frustrated over the recurring sins in my life. But Your Word says that once You saved me through Christ, sin no longer had any hold over me. Help me to submit myself to You, to resist the devil's wiles in Your power, and to rest in Your victory.

....

....

....

....

....

....

....

....

....

....

....

Submit yourselves therefore to God.
Resist the devil, and he will flee from you.

JAMES 4:7

Let not sin therefore reign in your mortal body, that ye should obey
it in the lusts thereof. Neither yield ye your members as instruments
of unrighteousness unto sin: but yield yourselves unto God, as those
that are alive from the dead, and your members as instruments of
righteousness unto God. For sin shall not have dominion over you:
for ye are not under the law, but under grace.

ROMANS 6:12–14

Trials

◆

The Bible warns us not to be surprised when trials come, but that doesn't make them any less difficult to bear. Some trials are the result of persecution; others are evidence of the broken world we live in—natural disasters, a sudden loss, chronic illnesses. As you look at these promises from God's Word, remember that He assures us that our trials have a purpose—when we walk with Him, troubled times transform us more and more into the image of Christ. In the midst of hardship, our Savior will provide us the strength and courage to endure with joy.

Wherein ye greatly rejoice, though now for a season, if need be, ye are in heaviness through manifold temptations: that the trial of your faith, being much more precious than of gold that perisheth, though it be tried with fire, might be found unto praise and honour and glory at the appearing of Jesus Christ.

1 Peter 1:6–7

Jesus, I pray as the apostle Paul did—I am troubled, perplexed, persecuted, cast down in the trial I'm in now, but not undone. Help me endure, to focus my hope on how Your glory will come out of this. In You is all the victory, and You are worthy of my trust.

....

....

....

....

....

....

....

....

....

....

....

We are troubled on every side, yet not distressed; we are perplexed, but not in despair; persecuted, but not forsaken; cast down, but not destroyed; always bearing about in the body the dying of the Lord Jesus, that the life also of Jesus might be made manifest in our body. For we which live are always delivered unto death for Jesus' sake, that the life also of Jesus might be made manifest in our mortal flesh.

2 CORINTHIANS 4:8–11

For whatsoever is born of God overcometh the world: and this is the victory that overcometh the world, even our faith. Who is he that overcometh the world, but he that believeth that Jesus is the Son of God?

1 JOHN 5:4–5

I know trials are not strange for Your people, Lord. The world doesn't understand Your ways and fights against them. Though my trial is hot and scorching, use it to melt away the impurities in my life, that I may be more like Christ and the world can see You in me.

....

....

....

....

....

....

....

....

....

Beloved, think it not strange concerning the fiery trial which is to try you, as though some strange thing happened unto you: but rejoice, inasmuch as ye are partakers of Christ's sufferings; that, when his glory shall be revealed, ye may be glad also with exceeding joy.

1 PETER 4:12–13

And I will bring the third part through the fire, and will refine them as silver is refined, and will try them as gold is tried: they shall call on my name, and I will hear them: I will say, It is my people: and they shall say, The LORD is my God.

ZECHARIAH 13:9

Father, in the midst of my trial, I need Your comfort.
I lean hard into Your promises—Your nearness, my identity
as Your beloved child. I both want to be faithful and want
the trial to be over, but as long as You have me in it,
help me to humbly trust You through it all.

....

....

....

....

....

....

....

....

*Blessed be God, even the Father of our Lord Jesus Christ,
the Father of mercies, and the God of all comfort; who comforteth
us in all our tribulation, that we may be able to comfort them
which are in any trouble, by the comfort wherewith we ourselves
are comforted of God. For as the sufferings of Christ abound
in us, so our consolation also aboundeth by Christ.*

2 CORINTHIANS 1:3–5

*But now thus saith the LORD that created thee, O Jacob, and he
that formed thee, O Israel, Fear not: for I have redeemed thee,
I have called thee by thy name; thou art mine. When thou passest
through the waters, I will be with thee; and through the rivers,
they shall not overflow thee: when thou walkest through the fire,
thou shalt not be burned; neither shall the flame kindle upon thee.*

ISAIAH 43:1–2

Unworthiness

When we don't function the way we want to—whether we are newly hurt or recovering—it's easy to look at the healthy "norm" and feel unworthy: "I'm so hard to be around. I'm such a burden." We might feel like we don't deserve others' love and attention. But Christ doesn't measure us by what we can accomplish physically or handle emotionally. He looks at us with the same love that moved Him to come to Earth to save us. These Bible promises show that you are complete, worthy, and accepted in Jesus—embrace His profound love when you feel unlovable.

Blessed be the God and Father of our Lord Jesus Christ, who hath blessed us with all spiritual blessings in heavenly places in Christ: according as he hath chosen us in him before the foundation of the world, that we should be holy and without blame before him in love: having predestinated us unto the adoption of children by Jesus Christ to himself, according to the good pleasure of his will, to the praise of the glory of his grace, wherein he hath made us accepted in the beloved. In whom we have redemption through his blood, the forgiveness of sins, according to the riches of his grace.

EPHESIANS 1:3–7

Jesus, I can't think of any reasons for You to choose me, but then You remind me it wasn't anything I did. It was just Your all-surpassing love—not something I can lose or change. Sink my roots in the deep soil of Your love so I can grow to new heights.

....
....
....
....
....
....
....
....
....
....
....
....

For by grace are ye saved through faith; and that not of yourselves:
it is the gift of God: not of works, lest any man should boast.
EPHESIANS 2:8–9

That Christ may dwell in your hearts by faith; that ye,
being rooted and grounded in love, may be able to comprehend
with all saints what is the breadth, and length, and depth,
and height; and to know the love of Christ, which passeth
knowledge, that ye might be filled with all the fulness of God.
EPHESIANS 3:17–19

Father, I feel like the prodigal son, asking if I could just
be a servant in Your house, but You embrace me and say,
"No, you are My child! I give the good things of My heart
to My children." Help me live in the sweet knowledge
of Your acceptance and lavish grace toward me!

....
....
....
....
....
....
....
....
....
....

*Know ye that the LORD he is God: it is he that hath made us,
and not we ourselves; we are his people, and the sheep of his pasture.*

PSALM 100:3

*For ye have not received the spirit of bondage again to fear; but ye have
received the Spirit of adoption, whereby we cry, Abba, Father. The Spirit
itself beareth witness with our spirit, that we are the children of God:
and if children, then heirs; heirs of God, and joint-heirs with Christ;
if so be that we suffer with him, that we may be also glorified together.*

ROMANS 8:15–17

Your love is relentless, Holy Father. You come and blow down the barriers I erected in my heart—"unworthy," "not worth others' attention," "screwup"—proclaiming, "You are Mine, and I rejoice over whom I have made, My redeemed, sought-out one!" Your song is loud and unapologetic—Your love is amazing, O Lord!

....

....

....

....

....

....

....

....

....

....

....

....

....

The LORD thy God in the midst of thee is mighty;
he will save, he will rejoice over thee with joy; he will
rest in his love, he will joy over thee with singing.

ZEPHANIAH 3:17

And they shall call them, The holy people, The redeemed of the LORD:
and thou shalt be called, Sought out, A city not forsaken.

ISAIAH 62:12

Vulnerability

◆

Nobody likes being seen as weak. When we are in pain, we can feel especially vulnerable in difficult situations or around other people. Though we try, we cannot shield our hearts with enough armor to keep out everything that threatens us. God knows our every vulnerable place, but He responds in tenderness when we show Him our hidden selves. He can give you the courage to ask others for what you need to feel safe and also give you the strength you need to persevere. May these Bible promises give you confidence in the grace God has for you!

Like as a father pitieth his children, so the LORD pitieth them that fear him. For he knoweth our frame; he remembereth that we are dust. As for man, his days are as grass: as a flower of the field, so he flourisheth. For the wind passeth over it, and it is gone; and the place thereof shall know it no more.

PSALM 103:13–16

When I want to retreat, to not have anyone ask me how I'm doing because I don't want to answer, Jesus, remind me of Your abundant grace, the gift that is enough no matter the lack I feel. Thank You for being gentle with my heart when it's raw and hurting.

....

....

....

....

....

....

....

....

....

....

....

....

....

....

....

And of his fulness have all we received, and grace for grace. For the law was given by Moses, but grace and truth came by Jesus Christ.

JOHN 1:16–17

But unto every one of us is given grace according to the measure of the gift of Christ.

EPHESIANS 4:7

Lord, there are times when I feel like every nerve is exposed to the words of others, my feelings threatening to crumble at any moment. But You are gracious. You hold me tenderly with Your strong and mighty hand. I bring these vulnerable days to You; thank You for taking care of me.

....
....
....
....
....
....
....
....
....

And therefore will the LORD wait, that he may be gracious unto you, and therefore will he be exalted, that he may have mercy upon you: for the LORD is a God of judgment: blessed are all they that wait for him. For the people shall dwell in Zion at Jerusalem: thou shalt weep no more: he will be very gracious unto thee at the voice of thy cry; when he shall hear it, he will answer thee.

ISAIAH 30:18–19

Thou hast also given me the shield of thy salvation: and thy right hand hath holden me up, and thy gentleness hath made me great.

PSALM 18:35

Father, sometimes it feels there is no privacy, no dignity left on this healing journey. In the worst moments I feel unprotected, exposed to everything. But Your Word promises that I am Yours, Your precious one. Shield me with Your love, Holy God; show me I am surrounded and safe.

....

....

....

....

....

....

....

....

....

....

....

*Nevertheless the foundation of God standeth sure,
having this seal, The Lord knoweth them that are his.*
2 TIMOTHY 2:19

*For I, saith the LORD, will be unto her a wall of fire round about,
and will be the glory in the midst of her. . . . For thus saith the LORD
of hosts; After the glory hath he sent me unto the nations which
spoiled you: for he that toucheth you toucheth the apple of his eye.*
ZECHARIAH 2:5, 8

Waiting

---

*S*o often, we find ourselves in the psalmist's position—we cry out to the Lord in our troubles and then wait for His answer. Though it's hard, waiting can become a holy practice where we intentionally turn away from worrying to set our hearts on Jesus and His deliverance. Still, sometimes we grow impatient or angry, or teeter on the edge of hopelessness. Thankfully, the Holy Spirit is gentle with us and able to minister to the needs of our hearts. These Bible promises show that our patience is well founded, because God promises He is faithful to answer our prayers.

But they that wait upon the LORD shall renew their strength; they shall mount up with wings as eagles; they shall run, and not be weary; and they shall walk, and not faint.

ISAIAH 40:31

I just want to be done with this journey, Lord. You have Your perfect plan, though, and Your Word encourages me to keep holding on, for I will see Your mercy in Your time. I don't know what form Your plan will take, but help me wait patiently for it, for You.

....

....

....

....

....

....

....

....

....

....

It is of the LORD's mercies that we are not consumed, because his compassions fail not. They are new every morning: great is thy faithfulness. The LORD is my portion, saith my soul; therefore will I hope in him. The LORD is good unto them that wait for him, to the soul that seeketh him. It is good that a man should both hope and quietly wait for the salvation of the LORD.

LAMENTATIONS 3:22–26

And it shall be said in that day, Lo, this is our God; we have waited for him, and he will save us: this is the LORD; we have waited for him, we will be glad and rejoice in his salvation.

ISAIAH 25:9

In the hours when I wait—for the wave of pain to pass, for the phone call, for my heart to quiet—let me wait for You. I look in expectation for Your grace—in tears, with praise—trusting Your deep love. Bind my heart together, Lord, so that waiting cannot break it!

....

....

....

....

....

....

....

....

....

....

I wait for the LORD, my soul doth wait, and in his word do I hope. My soul waiteth for the Lord more than they that watch for the morning: I say, more than they that watch for the morning. Let Israel hope in the LORD: for with the LORD there is mercy, and with him is plenteous redemption.

PSALM 130:5–7

Our soul waiteth for the LORD: he is our help and our shield. For our heart shall rejoice in him, because we have trusted in his holy name. Let thy mercy, O LORD, be upon us, according as we hope in thee.

PSALM 33:20–22

To think that waiting and courage can go hand in hand, Father—strengthen my heart in my waiting. Show me how to pray and keep trusting You, and protect me from looking enviously on what You've given others. You've given me Yourself—a precious gift! Thank You that I can rest in You.

....

....

....

....

....

....

....

....

....

....

....

Wait on the LORD: be of good courage, and he shall strengthen thine heart: wait, I say, on the LORD.

PSALM 27:14

Trust in the LORD, and do good; so shalt thou dwell in the land, and verily thou shalt be fed. . . . Rest in the LORD, and wait patiently for him: fret not thyself because of him who prospereth in his way, because of the man who bringeth wicked devices to pass.

PSALM 37:3, 7

Wisdom

———◆———

$\mathcal{D}$uring the healing and recovery process, we have so many questions. "Which doctors should I listen to? How do I handle my finances? Is this new procedure worth the risk?" The Bible says that the fear of the Lord is the beginning of knowledge. Whatever situation we're in, we are wisest when we depend on wisdom's true source, our heavenly Father. Applying the Bible's timeless truth to our lives and seeking His wisdom in prayer is a good start for answering the hard questions. Take heart! These Bible promises show that God generously gives wisdom to those who seek it.

If any of you lack wisdom, let him ask of God, that giveth to all men liberally, and upbraideth not; and it shall be given him. But let him ask in faith, nothing wavering. For he that wavereth is like a wave of the sea driven with the wind and tossed. For let not that man think that he shall receive any thing of the Lord.

JAMES 1:5–7

God of all wisdom, thank You for Your Word, for it gives life to those who listen and learn from it. Though oftentimes the voices of the world clamor around me, let the ear of my heart be listening for You—Your wisdom is better than anything the world offers.

....

....

....

....

....

....

....

....

....

....

....

....

The grass withereth, the flower fadeth:
but the word of our God shall stand for ever.
ISAIAH 40:8

Happy is the man that findeth wisdom, and the man that getteth
understanding. For the merchandise of it is better than the
merchandise of silver, and the gain thereof than fine gold.
PROVERBS 3:13–14

Lord, I know my wants can cloud my judgment, as can the trials of the healing process. Please renew my mind, training my discernment through the Word to recognize Your ways. No matter what decisions I must make, I trust Your promise to guide me in the way I need to go.

....

....

....

....

....

....

....

....

....

....

....

....

....

....

And be not conformed to this world: but be ye transformed by the renewing of your mind, that ye may prove what is that good, and acceptable, and perfect, will of God.

Romans 12:2

Thou shalt guide me with thy counsel, and afterward receive me to glory.

Psalm 73:24

Holy Spirit, I'm so thankful You know everything and that You are generous to grant me wisdom when I ask. I humbly come before You, my heart open and teachable—please fill me with the understanding I need to make wise decisions, and lead me forward on this healing journey.

....

....

....

....

....

....

But as it is written, Eye hath not seen, nor ear heard, neither have entered into the heart of man, the things which God hath prepared for them that love him. But God hath revealed them unto us by his Spirit: for the Spirit searcheth all things, yea, the deep things of God. For what man knoweth the things of a man, save the spirit of man which is in him? even so the things of God knoweth no man, but the Spirit of God. Now we have received, not the spirit of the world, but the spirit which is of God; that we might know the things that are freely given to us of God.

1 CORINTHIANS 2:9–12

Give instruction to a wise man, and he will be yet wiser: teach a just man, and he will increase in learning. The fear of the LORD is the beginning of wisdom: and the knowledge of the holy is understanding. For by me thy days shall be multiplied, and the years of thy life shall be increased.

PROVERBS 9:9–11

Worry

*A*s productive as it feels, worrying doesn't calm us. Instead, it lets fear seep into the corners of our hearts. We can't know for sure how the next phase of our recovery will go or whether our estranged friend will accept our apology, but God does. Nothing happens without His knowledge. He knows we're tempted to worry, so He filled His Word with these promises— He has a plan, He will provide, and His greatness can overcome anything we face. Stand secure in these Bible promises that testify to the certainty of His great love and care for us!

Therefore I say unto you, Take no thought for your life, what ye shall eat, or what ye shall drink; nor yet for your body, what ye shall put on. Is not the life more than meat, and the body than raiment? Behold the fowls of the air: for they sow not, neither do they reap, nor gather into barns; yet your heavenly Father feedeth them. Are ye not much better than they? Which of you by taking thought can add one cubit unto his stature? And why take ye thought for raiment? Consider the lilies of the field, how they grow; they toil not, neither do they spin: and yet I say unto you, that even Solomon in all his glory was not arrayed like one of these.

Matthew 6:25–29

Jesus, I need Your peace! My worries weigh heavy on me, disturbing my rest and making my heart race. Here they are; take them. Instead of worrying, help me spend time thanking You for Your blessings. . .reminding my soul of how You have sustained me in the past.

....

....

....

....

....

....

....

....

....

....

....

....

Be careful for nothing; but in every thing by prayer and supplication with thanksgiving let your requests be made known unto God. And the peace of God, which passeth all understanding, shall keep your hearts and minds through Christ Jesus.

PHILIPPIANS 4:6–7

Cast thy burden upon the LORD, and he shall sustain thee: he shall never suffer the righteous to be moved.

PSALM 55:22

Lord, I know I shouldn't worry, but it's so hard when there is so much uncertainty. Encourage me to remember that You are with me, You already know my needs, and You go ahead of me into the future. Help me rest in these promises when the difficult things are piling up around me.

....

....

....

....

....

....

....

....

Therefore take no thought, saying, What shall we eat? or, What shall we drink? or, Wherewithal shall we be clothed? (For after all these things do the Gentiles seek:) for your heavenly Father knoweth that ye have need of all these things. But seek ye first the kingdom of God, and his righteousness; and all these things shall be added unto you. Take therefore no thought for the morrow: for the morrow shall take thought for the things of itself. Sufficient unto the day is the evil thereof.

Matthew 6:31–34

Let your conversation be without covetousness; and be content with such things as ye have: for he hath said, I will never leave thee, nor forsake thee. So that we may boldly say, The Lord is my helper, and I will not fear what man shall do unto me.

Hebrews 13:5–6

Choosing not to worry feels almost impossible, Father, with the struggles I have. You can help me replace worry with something better, though—rejoicing, which refocuses my heart on You and Your abundance. Because You strengthen me, in trust I can open my mouth to praise, knowing You are my salvation.

He shall not be afraid of evil tidings:
his heart is fixed, trusting in the LORD.
PSALM 112:7

Although the fig tree shall not blossom, neither shall fruit be in the vines; the labour of the olive shall fail, and the fields shall yield no meat; the flock shall be cut off from the fold, and there shall be no herd in the stalls: yet I will rejoice in the LORD, I will joy in the God of my salvation. The LORD God is my strength, and he will make my feet like hinds' feet, and he will make me to walk upon mine high places.
HABAKKUK 3:17–19

LIKE PRAYER JOURNALS?

My Prayer Journal: Peaceful Moments to Bless Your Heart

What better way to guarantee a peaceful day than to spend time in prayer? *My Prayer Journal: Peaceful Moments to Bless Your Heart* encourages women to do just that—to set aside a few minutes each day for quiet time with God. Dozens of soul-soothing prayers are accompanied by inspiring scripture selections and generous journaling space.

Spiral Bound / 978-1-68322-313-9 / $7.99

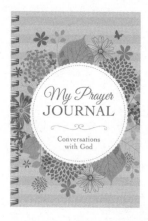

My Prayer Journal: Conversations with God

What better way to guarantee a good day than to spend time in prayer? *My Prayer Journal: Conversations with Go*d encourages women to do just that—to set aside just a few minutes each day for quiet time with God. Dozens of faith-building prayers are accompanied by inspiring scripture selections and generous journaling space.

Spiral Bound / 978-1-68322-120-3 / $7.99